SHERMAN FIREFLY
VS
TIGER

Normandy 1944

STEPHEN A HART

First published in Great Britain in 2007 by Osprey Publishing,
Midland House, West Way, Botley, Oxford OX2 0PH, UK
44-02 23rd St, Suite 219, Long Island City, NY 11101, USA
Email: info@ospreypublishing.com

Osprey Publishing is part of the Osprey Group.

A CIP catalogue record for this book is available from the British Library

ISBN: 978 1 84603 150 2

Page layout by Myriam Bell
Cover artwork, three-views and cutaway gun artwork by Jim Laurier
Battlescene by Howard Gerrard
Index by Alan Thatcher
Typeset in Adobe Garamond and ITC Conduit
Maps by Peter Bull Art Studio
Originated by PDQ Digital Media Solutions
Printed in China through Bookbuilders

11 12 13 14 15   15 14 13 12 11 10 9 8 7 6

The Woodland Trust
Osprey Publishing is supporting the Woodland Trust, the UK's leading woodland
conservation charity, by funding the dedication of trees.

Artist's note
Readers may care to note that the original painting from which the battlescene colour plate in
this book was prepared is available for private sale. All reproduction copyright whatsoever is
retained by the Publishers. All enquiries should be addressed to:

Howard Gerrard, 11 Oaks Road, Tenterden, Kent TN30 6RD

The Publishers regret that they can enter into no correspondence upon this matter.

www.ospreypublishing.com

Imperial War Museum Collections
Many of the photos in this book come from the Imperial
War Museum's huge collections which cover all aspects of
conflict involving Britain and the Commonwealth since
the start of the twentieth century. These rich resources
are available online to search, browse and buy at:
www.iwmcollections.org.uk. In addition to Collections
Online, you can visit the Visitor Rooms where you can
explore over 8 million photographs, thousands of hours
of moving images, the largest sound archive of its kind
in the world, thousands of diaries and letters written
by people in wartime, and a huge reference library.
To make an appointment, call (020) 7416 5320,
or e-mail mail@iwm.org.uk.

www.iwm.org.uk

CONTENTS

INTRODUCTION

The German Tiger heavy tank is today the most famous tank of World War II, if not one of the most famous tanks in history. Introduced in mid-1942, the Tiger featured extremely thick armour, providing it with what was at that time a formidable level of battlefield survivability. The Tiger also mounted a powerful long-barrelled 88mm gun that could at normal combat ranges defeat virtually every enemy tank then in existence. Germany's Tiger tanks dominated the battlefields of Europe for at least the next two years, striking fear into those Allied crews unfortunate enough to encounter them on the battlefield; many such crews did not survive these invariably brief and bloody actions. Although few in quantity, the relatively small numbers of Tigers available allowed the German forces to slow down the rising tide of Allied battlefield success for longer than they would have been able to otherwise.

By late summer 1944, however, the mighty Tiger was nearing its swansong. This period was the last time that the famous Tiger spearheaded Germany's defensive battles in any significant numbers. In August 1944, Tiger production ended in favour of the even more formidable King Tiger, which featured better-sloped armour and an even more powerful, longer-barrelled 88mm gun. With Tiger production halted, the inevitable attrition of combat meant that the Germans could only deploy the Tiger in decreasing numbers. This attritional process was speeded up that summer by the arrival on the battlefield of a new generation of potent Allied tanks that could, for the first time in the war, take on the Tiger and win. For this very task, the British had developed the Firefly, an up-gunned variant of the standard American-designed M4 Sherman medium tank. Instead of the 75mm gun of the standard Sherman, however, the Firefly mounted a potent 17-pounder gun that made it a deadly opponent for even the heavily armoured Tiger at normal combat ranges. Outperforming the 88mm L/56 gun of the Tiger, the theoretical penetrative power of the Firefly's 17-pounder only came close to being matched by the 88 L/71 gun mounted by the King Tiger, which was then only just coming into service.

This struggle for armoured supremacy between the Firefly tanks deployed on the one side by the British, Canadian and Polish armies, and on the other by Germany's Tiger tanks, was demonstrated most obviously during the summer 1944 battle for Normandy. During the two months of bitter combat that followed the Allied D-Day landings on 6 June 1944, the Allies painfully fought their way slowly inland in the face of fierce German resistance. Continued Allied offensive determination, however, gradually began to bear fruit during early August, as Germany's defensive resilience finally began to crumble. Indeed, by 8 August 1944, the fate of the entire German front in Normandy hung in the balance after powerful Allied offensives had torn it open in several places.

It was at one of these breaches, south of Caen, on the early afternoon of 8 August 1944, that the famous German Panzer ace SS-Hauptsturmführer (Captain) Michael Wittmann led his troop of four Tigers in a desperate charge north towards the Allied lines. Awaiting this scratch force was a mass of Allied armour, which included a number of Fireflies. Advancing north, Wittmann's Tigers blundered into a classic tank ambush. In the course of this brief, bloody engagement, the fire of just one Firefly accounted for three of Wittmann's Tigers. As Wittmann's tank exploded after being hit, the famed German Panzer ace, who had proved such a scourge to the Allies in Normandy, met the warrior's death that befitted his military career. This combat episode provides bountiful testimony to the awesome killing power of the Sherman Firefly, the Tiger tank destroyer extraordinaire.

This view of a Sherman Firefly, taken in Putanges, Normandy, on 20 August 1944, shows the sheer length of the tank's 17-pounder gun barrel. (IWM B9477)

CHRONOLOGY

1942

20 April   Trials held between the VK4501(P) and VK4501(H) Tiger prototypes at Rastenburg in front of Hitler in honour of his 53rd birthday.

20 Aug   The first four main production run Tigers completed.

29 Aug   First Tiger tank enters combat near Leningrad.

1943

March   Michael Wittmann takes command of his first Tiger tank.

1944

6 January   First Sherman Firefly completed.

February   First King Tiger tank completed; thereafter this increasingly replaced the Tiger in German heavy tank units.

This photograph shows the first prototype Firefly, chassis T148350, which was fitted with a wooden mock-up 17-pounder gun. This photograph was taken in early January 1944 at Chertsey in Surrey. (TTM 2995/B/3)

31 May   Some 342 Fireflies completed; most delivered to Montgomery's 21st Army Group for D-Day landings.

The first Firefly tanks to land on D-Day did so in the follow-up waves, from large Landing Ship Tanks (LSTs). Here a Firefly from the 7th Armoured Division, stowed with all sorts of extra equipment including a ladder on the left hull side, disembarks onto the beach. (IWM B5130)

From spring 1944 onwards the Tiger was replaced in German heavy battalions by the improved Panzer VI Model B King Tiger tank. The King Tiger, as this frontal view shows, featured better-sloped armour and an even more potent 71-calibre long 88mm gun. (Ken Bell/ PA-115744)

6 June	D-Day: Allied forces land on the coast of Normandy, in German-occupied France.
13 June	Wittmann's Tigers routs elements of the British 7th Armoured Division at Villers Bocage.
7–8 Aug	Allied *Totalize* offensive commences.
8 Aug	Michael Wittmann's Tiger destroyed by Sherman Firefly; Wittmann is killed.
Late Aug	Last Tiger tank out of a total production run of 1,349 completed by Henschel.

This top view of a Firefly shows well the length of the barrel, the distinctive egg-shaped muzzle brake, the large locker on the turret rear that housed the radio; the large circular commander's cupola in the right turret roof; and the unusually positioned square loader's hatch. (TTM 2995/B/1)

1945

Early May	The last Tiger tanks still operational – probably fewer than 30 – surrender as Germany's armed forces capitulate.
Late May	Last Sherman Firefly manufactured.

The Tiger was a squat, angular tank that sported very thick (but not well-sloped) armour and a potent long-barrelled 88mm gun. The standard 75mm-gunned Sherman stood little chance of knocking out a Tiger, even at close range, whereas the Firefly could penetrate the Tiger's armour from any direction at normal combat ranges. This Tiger was knocked out at Tosters, France, on 30 August 1944. (Harold G. Aiken/Library and Archives/Canada/PA-114159)

One of the last Firefly actions of the war. A tank of the 7th Armoured Division enters the centre of Hamburg, passing the memorial to the Great War, on 4 May 1945. Note the closed-style road wheels and the foliage liberally added by the crew for camouflage. (IWM BU5284)

DESIGN AND DEVELOPMENT

THE TIGER

Introduced in mid-1942, the Tiger can trace its direct development back to 1941 and its indirect antecedents to 1937. During 1937–40, the Germans carried out development work on a tank heavier than their then heaviest tank – the Panzer IV. By 1940, this programme for a 29.5 ton tank – designated the VK3001 – had produced several prototype designs, named the Breakthrough Tanks 1 and 2 (DW1 and 2) and the VK3001(H). The DW1 chassis, developed by the German armaments firm of Henschel, sported 50mm thick armour plates and was powered by a 280bhp Maybach ML 120 engine. Its suspension featured the typical German torsion bar suspension. During 1939 Henschel produced its DW2 design. This tank married a modified DW1 chassis to a Krupp-designed turret that mounted the 7.5cm KwK L/24 gun used in the Panzer IV. Finally, during 1940 Henschel produced the VK3001(H) design. This was a turret-less chassis which incorporated a novel running-gear arrangement based on interleaved wheels. The 30-ton VK3001(H), which featured 600mm-thick armour plates, was powered by a 300bhp Maybach HL 116 six-cylinder engine and could obtain a maximum road speed of 21mph.

During 1940, the Henschel firm also began work on the heavier VK6501(H) design – an enlarged, up-armoured and larger engined version of the Panzer IV designed to fulfil the Army's future 65 ton KV6501/Panzer requirement. This massive design was to be powered by a 12-cylinder 600bhp Maybach HL 224 engine. Developmental work on this design did not progress any further, however, because the Army Weapons Department was happy with the Panzer IV as its heaviest vehicle. Nevertheless, these design efforts influenced the subsequent work that would lead to to the production of the Tiger.

The rival armaments firm of Porsche, meanwhile, had begun to develop a heavy tank designated the VK4501(P) – seemingly at Hitler's request and without formal contracts from the Weapons Department. From spring 1941, Krupp began to collaborate with Porsche on this project, by supplying the latter with its recently developed 88mm KwK 36 L/56 tank gun – a modified version of the famous 88mm (3.46in) anti-aircraft gun. The long-barrelled Krupp tank gun delivered an impressive anti-tank capability by achieving a high muzzle velocity for its rounds. The effort the Germans devoted to heavy tank design remained dilatory until 26 May 1941, when a meeting of experts chaired by Hitler reviewed future German tank development strategy. At this meeting, the Führer demanded that a well-armoured German heavy tank be developed that would out-gun any enemy tank it might encounter. Future development work should proceed on the basis of a vehicle that sported 100mm thick frontal armour and a gun that could penetrate 100mm of armour at a range of 1500m. The Führer thus ordered that the work already undertaken by the firms of Porsche and Henschel should be accelerated so that each could construct six prototype vehicles by summer 1942.

These developmental programmes received another major impetus during the second half of 1941, as the German Army reacted to the shock experienced when its Panzers encountered two unexpectedly formidable Soviet AFV designs – the T-34 medium and KV heavy tanks. These modern Soviet tanks outclassed all German tanks

Henschel's VK3001(H) design, seen here in early 1940. This design departed from traditional German design by the introduction of a novel running-gear arrangement based on interleaved road wheels. This successful arrangement subsequently led Henschel to use this type of arrangement in their Tiger prototype, the VK4501(H). (TTM 6612/G/3)

then in existence, including their heaviest vehicle, the Panzer IV. This realization prompted the Germans to begin developing new medium- and heavy-tank designs. Work commenced simultaneously on a number of designs during 1941–42, but eventually these efforts coalesced during 1942–43 to produce a new generation of heavier, more powerfully armed and better protected tanks – the Panzer V 'Panther' and the Panzer VI Model E 'Tiger'.

During 1942, however, these reinvigorated German efforts to develop a new heavy tank remained dogged by controversy. Hitler wanted the future heavy tank to mount an 8.8cm gun – either the KwK 36 or a version of the new and yet more powerful Rheinmetal 8.8cm Flak 41. After experimentation, Porsche concluded that the latter weapon was not suitable for mounting in the turret it was then developing. The Weapons Department, on the other hand, felt that mounting such a large gun in a tank (which would need to be large to accommodate a turret with a sufficiently wide turret ring to house the gun) would render the vehicle too heavy and immobile. The Department felt that the future heavy tank should mount a smaller 60mm or 70mm tapered-bore gun. This was a gun with an interior bore to the barrel that narrows towards the muzzle. This narrowing squeezes the special Tungsten steel round into the rifling on the inside of the barrel, enabling the round to be fired with greater muzzle velocity and accuracy, but crucially from a smaller gun. Tungsten steel, however, was an alloy that was already scarce and in much demand within the German war economy. The wrangling associated with this dispute led to the simultaneous commencement of work on two separate prototype heavy tank programmes.

The Germans contracted one project, designated VK3601(H), to Henschel based on a specification for a 32.7-ton vehicle that mounted a tapered-bore 60mm or 70mm gun. Meanwhile, Porsche finally received formal contracts to produce the heavier VK4501(P) design, which mounted Krupp's 88mm tank gun. By mid-1941 Henschel

BELOW The mammoth symbol on the tank is the tactical symbol for the unit schwere Panzer Abteilungen 502 (s. Pz Abt 502) – Heavy Tank Battalion 502. This was the first heavy tank battalion to be formed during the summer 1942. It was also the first unit to see action on the Eastern Front at Leningrad in August 1942. It was an inaudacious start. Several of the tanks got bogged down in the marshy terrain or simply broke down. The unit was later posted to France where it saw action from July 1944 onwards. It was re-formed in early 1945 as S. Pz Abt 511 and refitted with King Tigers. The unit eventually surrendered to the Soviets in May 1945.

TIGER SIDE-VIEW

8.24m

The VK4501(P), or Porsche Tiger, mounted the same Krupp turret with its 88mm gun as the rival Henschel design, but this was positioned further forward than in the Henschel tank, making the Porsche design front-heavy. In this view the turret has been traversed so that the gun faces towards the rear.

had produced seven prototype VK3601(H) tanks that featured thick frontal armour and interleaved road wheels. However, the Germans then concluded that such was the demand for and scarcity of Tungsten steel, that the tapered-bore gun central to the Henschel project was no longer feasible. The only way that the smaller Henschel heavy tank could compete with the heavier rival Porsche one in tank-killing capability was to employ tapered-bore technology; with this ruled out, Henschel had no choice but to abandon the VK3601(H) programme. The Germans, however, did not wish to waste the valuable design work Henschel had put into this project. Consequently, the Weapons Department contracted Henschel to develop a 41-ton heavy tank, the VK4501(H). Henschel decided to develop an enlarged version of its VK3601 that would mount the same 88mm tank gun featured in the rival VK4501(P) design. By late 1941, therefore, both Henschel and Porsche were now working on rival 41-ton heavy-tank designs that mounted the same gun.

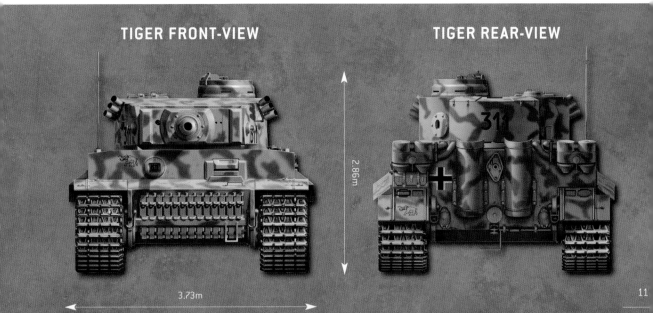

TIGER FRONT-VIEW

TIGER REAR-VIEW

2.86m

3.73m

By April 1942, Porsche and Henschel had completed their first prototype VK4501(P) and VK4501(H) heavy tanks, now generally referred to as the Porsche-Tiger and Henschel-Tiger, respectively. These rival designs had certain common features; most notably they mounted the same Krupp-designed turret that featured the 8.8cm KwK L/56 gun and the co-axial MG 34 machine gun. Both designs also had a ball-mounted bow machine gun and sported heavy armour up to a maximum of 120mm thick on the turret mantlet. Moreover, both tanks weighed around 53.6 tons, markedly above the original specification, because the German hierarchy increased the project's required levels of armour during the design process. Beyond this commonality, however, the two rivals were quite different.

The VK4501(P) was powered by two air-cooled Simmering-Graz-Pauker 320bhp engines that drove the tank through a series of dynamos and electric motors; the vehicle's drive mechanism was thus of petro-electric type, a typical Porsche arrangement. The VK4501(P) also featured a novel suspension that comprised six steel double road wheels suspended in pairs from longitudinal torsion bars. Because of its high fuel consumption, however, the tank could only achieve a disappointing operational range of just 50km. The tank also featured a low squat chassis with the angular Krupp-turret located well forward, which resulted in the long 88mm gun overhanging the front of the vehicle to a conspicuous degree. This made the design very heavy at the front end, and consequently the tank was prone to get bogged down in soft terrain. Nevertheless, during April 1942, before this design had even been evaluated, Porsche received contracts for 90 tanks to be delivered during the period January–April 1943.

Several features differentiated Henschel's VK4501(H) tank from its Porsche rival. The Henschel tank mounted the identical Krupp turret but in the centre of the vehicle, not at the front. This arrangement reduced the degree to which the main gun overhung the front of the vehicle, rendering it less front-heavy. The Henschel tank's running gear featured the same novel interleaved road-wheel arrangement used in the

The first of the Tiger experimental series, the VK4501(H) V1 is seen here at the assembly hall of Henschel's Kassel factory in April 1942. It differed only marginally from the subsequent production Tiger design. (TTM 2395/B/5)

earlier VK3001(H). Unlike the Porsche design, the Henschel tank's suspension was based on the typical German arrangement of lateral torsion bars. Moreover the tank's hull superstructure was also wider and more angular than that of the Porsche tank. The VK4501(H) also featured a single, rear-located 642bhp Maybach petrol engine, and its fuel tanks provided it with a marginally better cross-country operating range than its Porsche rival. The Henschel tank also featured a hydraulically-controlled pre-selected eight-speed Maybach Olvar OG40 gearbox and semi-automatic transmission.

To evaluate which of the two rival designs was superior, the Germans held a field trial in front of Hitler and other top Nazi officials at Rastenburg on 20 April 1942 – the Führer's 53rd birthday. When this and subsequent competitive trials had been completed, the Army concluded – despite Hitler's prejudiced favouritism for Porsche – that the Henschel model was marginally better than the Porsche; the greatest advantages were Henschel's superior engine power reliability and vehicle mobility. The Weapons Department also concluded that the Henschel tank was better suited for mass production than its rival – an important consideration for an already hard-pressed German war economy.

Hitler demanded that the new tank be committed to action as soon as possible. In July 1942 the Weapons Department contracted Henschel to mass produce this tank under the designation Panzer VI Model E Tiger (later simplified to Panzer VI Tiger). Simultaneously, the Department cancelled the contracts already awarded to Porsche for its 90 Porsche-Tigers. Not wishing to waste these 90 partially constructed chassis, however, the Germans subsequently used them to produce an improvised heavy-tank destroyer designated 'Elephant'. In addition to its test vehicle (designated Experimental Series Panzer VI H1), the first two Tiger tanks Henschel produced in early August were two pre-production vehicles. Henschel then completed the first four tanks in the main production run on 20 August. These were rushed off to the Eastern Front on 29 August 1942. Thereafter arriving on the battlefields of Europe in greater numbers, the Tiger soon earned a fearsome reputation that it maintained well into the second half of 1944.

THE FIREFLY

The Sherman Firefly, in contrast, did not enter combat until June 1944, by which time Tiger production would shortly be terminated. By late 1943, the American-designed M4 Sherman had become the British Army's standard medium tank, equipping many of its armoured brigades. The Sherman was the first effective dual-purpose Allied tank that could perform adequately both the infantry support role (which required a heavily armoured tank) and the exploitation role (which required a fast and mobile, and thus lightly armoured, tank).

The M4 Sherman was a five-man tank in the 31–35 ton range, depending on the mark, which in British service was designated Sherman I through to V. These tanks either mounted the 75mm American M3 gun, or the 76mm American M1 gun, together with one co-axial and one bow machine gun. The tank sported sloped frontal armour that was up to 76mm thick, together with 38mm side plates. Powered by a rear-located Chrysler, Wright, GMC or Ford engine that produced 400–443bhp, the Sherman could achieve a maximum speed of 36kph on roads and 22kph cross-country. The Sherman's running gear comprised three pairs of bogie road wheels, based on the Vertical Volute Spring Suspension (VVSS) arrangement. The Sherman also featured a five-speed synchromesh gearbox and clutch-and-brake transmission; this produced a rather crude steering system in comparison to the sophisticated (if fault-prone) twin-radius system employed in the Tiger.

However, combat experience in the Western Desert and Italy during 1942–43 had shown that British tanks were vulnerable to the latest Panzers. The long-barrelled 75mm guns of the new Panzer IV Special and Panther inflicted heavy losses on British armour, as did the Tiger's even more potent 88mm gun. The latter could knock out British tanks at such long range that the Tiger remained impervious to return fire. This situation led the War Office to consider how to up-gun their existing tanks so that they could knock out any German tank at a range up to 1,300m. The obvious weapon for this was the Royal Ordnance 17-pounder anti-tank gun, which had an established track-record as a tank killer. Firing armoured piercing rounds, the gun could penetrate 172mm armour at 914m range – sufficient to penetrate even the Tiger's formidable gun-mantlet armour.

During late 1943, the British first attempted to mount this fearsome weapon on the Cromwell tank chassis. Entering service in March 1944, much later than expected, the resulting A30 Challenger tank remained an unsatisfactory expedient. The Challenger featured a tall turret, which was required to mount the gun's tall mechanism, as well as levels of armour protection inadequate for the battlefields of 1944. As the War Office's dissatisfaction with the delayed Challenger programme

BELOW A Firefly from the Sherman-equipped armoured regiment 1 Northamptonshire Yeomanry. Led by Lt-Col D. Foster, the regiment fielded three squadrons – 'A', 'B' and 'C'. Most of the regiment's tanks bore distinctive names. 'A' Squadrons were named after Soviet towns. This is tank No.16 'Kursk'.

FIREFLY SIDE-VIEW

KURSK

T 148725

7.82m

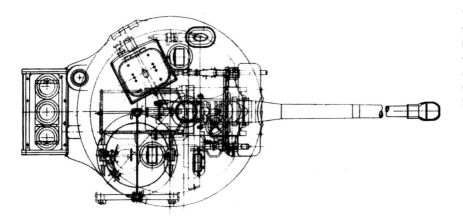

This technical diagram of the turret arrangements shows how cramped the turret was when the large breech mechanism of the 17-pounder was introduced into the small Sherman turret. (TTM)

grew during late 1943, its thoughts increasingly turned to the issue of whether the 17-pounder could be successfully mounted in the Sherman. This latter possibility had been first entertained back in late August 1943, but no official action to investigate the matter was authorized until early October.

The Ministry of Supply's Tank Department remained sceptical that the gun could be mounted effectively in the existing 75mm-equipped Sherman. The existing 17-pounder anti-tank gun featured large and cumbersome cylinders located both above and below the barrel to absorb the gun's powerful recoil; this made the gun too tall to fit into the compact Sherman turret. The sheer force of the recoil would also take up a large proportion of the already limited available space in the Sherman turret. However, back in summer 1943 the Royal Armoured Corps Gunnery School at Lulworth had already undertaken some unofficial experiments with mounting the gun in a modified Sherman turret, which convinced them the proposition was both a feasible and economic one.

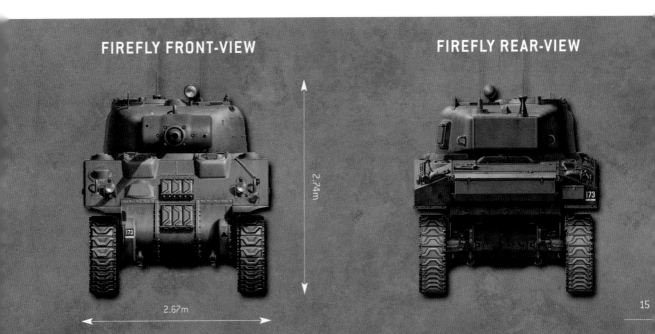

FIREFLY FRONT-VIEW

FIREFLY REAR-VIEW

2.74m

2.67m

With the War Office won over by these arguments, it issued a contract for the design of a modified version of the 17-pounder, designated the Mark IV, which would fit in the Sherman turret. This design was based on the earlier Lulworth Cove experiments, which had employed the expertise of a Vickers engineer, W.G.K Wilbourne, who was attached to the Department of Tank Design. During late autumn 1943, British engineers produced the redesigned gun, which featured a modified barrel base in front of the breech that shortened the weapon's recoil in its cradle. This redesign also left the gun with more suitably arranged recoil cylinders and a modified mount. During late December 1943, the new gun and mount were successfully tested. Such was the haste with which the War Office now embraced this project, that within a few days of the trials being completed, the gun and mount were fitted into a modified Sherman V chassis. This vehicle is said to have been completed at Woolwich on 31 December 1943. On 6 January 1944, trials began on the new vehicle, now designated the 17-pounder Sherman. This tank was differentiated from other variants with the suffix "C" after the mark, but did not use the the name Firefly. For whatever reason, the first units to receive the new tank used this name and since 1945 it has become the common designation for the tank.

By January 1944, the War Office was desperate to mount a more effective tank-killing weapon in the ubiquitous Sherman – not least because the Allied invasion of Nazi-occupied France was only a few months away. Fortunately, the War Office was entirely satisfied with the trials undertaken by the first Firefly in early January. The design offered a quick and easy-to-accomplish expedient that would deliver reasonable numbers over the ensuing months. The War Office immediately placed production orders with the Royal Ordnance Factories at Leeds, Cardiff, Woolwich and Hayes for an initial batch of several hundred Fireflies to be completed as soon as possible. The speed of the process by which the Firefly was designed, tested and manufactured owed much to the rapidly growing support at the highest political levels that emerged for the up-gunning of the Sherman. On 12 January 1944 Prime Minister Winston Churchill accorded the Firefly programme 'the highest priority … [within] the whole munitions programme'.

The first British attempt to mount the existing 17-pounder gun in a tank produced the A30 Challenger, based on the Cromwell chassis. This view shows a 2nd Northants Yeomanry tank in Normandy on 17 August 1944.
The Challenger was an unsatisfactory expedient that suffered from inadequate levels of armour protection.
(IWM B9331)

TECHNICAL SPECIFICATIONS

THE TIGER

The first 250 Tigers manufactured by Henschel's Kassel factory between August 1942 and April 1943 formed a distinct batch. The standard Tiger tank was a large and angular vehicle – an unimpressed Lieutenant Otto Carius described it as 'plump' – not dissimilar to the smaller Panzer IV in appearance. Weighing 55 tons, the Tiger mounted the same potent long-barrelled 8.8cm KwK 36 L/56 main gun as the prototype. Using an armour-piercing round, this accurate gun could penetrate the side or rear armour of a Sherman V or VC Firefly at a staggering 3,500m and puncture it frontally at 1,800m. In contrast, the standard 75mm-gunned Sherman could only puncture the Tiger's side armour at 100m, and could not even penetrate the Tiger frontally at point-blank range. The Tiger typically engaged an enemy tank at 800–1,200m range, although lucky kills at 2,000m were not unknown; the gun could even fire a High Explosive (HE) round 8,000m. The Tiger carried 92 rounds for its main gun, usually a 50–50 mix of Armour Piercing Capped Ballistic Capped (APCBC) and HE rounds. Less commonly, the Tiger carried a few Armour Piercing Composite Rigid (APCR) and High Explosive Anti-Tank (HEAT) rounds.

The Tiger possessed very thick high-quality homogenous armour that ranged from 120mm-thick mantlet armour to 80–82mm-thick side and rear plates. This armour provided excellent battlefield survivability, even if – in comparison with later tanks –

it was not well-sloped. Manned by a crew of five, the tank was powered by a 642bhp Maybach HL210 petrol engine. Yet despite its immense size, the tank developed a satisfactory degree of mobility, obtaining top road and off-road speeds of 38kph and 20kph, respectively. A surprised Lieutenant Otto Carius discovered that the Tiger 'drove just like a car'. The vehicle devoured petrol, however, and thus its fuel tanks only enabled it to travel a paltry 57km off-road before it needed to refuel. It was able to move satisfactorily cross-country thanks to its unusually wide battle tracks, which ran on six interleaved layers of road wheels. When fitted with these battle tracks, however, the Tiger was too wide to be transported on a standard German railway flat car. To solve this problem the Germans designed the Tiger to use a two-track system. When

A Tiger is positioned upright on its rear hull in an assembly plant. The view of its underside shows well the interleaved road-wheel arrangement, which featured six layers of wheels on each side, around which the tracks revolved. The combined width of both tracks is virtually the same as the width of the tank's hull floor. The outer layer of wheels was removed when the tank was fitted with its narrower transportation tracks. (TTM 1636/C/3)

in action, the Tiger used its wide battle tracks. When it needed to be transported by rail, the crew removed these tracks and the outer layer of road wheels, and fitted narrower transport tracks. The Tiger was also too heavy to cross many European bridges, so it was fitted with wading equipment that allowed it to move submerged along the bed of a river.

In total, between August 1942 and August 1944, Henschel produced 1,349 Tigers, an unimpressive total for a 24-month production run. This low figure reflected the high cost and significant time – more than twice that needed for a Panther – that had to be expended to produce a tank as large, technically complex and well engineered as the Tiger. Yet the Tiger's combination of lethal firepower, superb battlefield survivability and adequate mobility meant that it dominated the battlefield during 1942–44. From summer 1944 onwards, however, it began to meet its match in better-armed and better-armoured Allied rivals such as the Firefly, the Soviet Josef Stalin heavy tanks and the American Pershing tanks.

The Tiger's undoubted battlefield prowess, however, did not mean that the design was without weaknesses. The tank's transmission was prone to breakdown if preventative maintenance was not carried out regularly; it needed a high level of general technical maintenance; ice tended to freeze on the interleaved road wheels; and it was extremely difficult to recover a disabled Tiger from the battlefield. Despite these flaws, the Tiger soon became the German tank most feared by Allied units. It continued to spearhead Germany's elite heavy-tank units until the latter half of 1944, after which it was increasingly replaced by the even more formidably armoured and gunned King Tiger. Nevertheless, Tigers continued to give sterling battlefield service, albeit in dwindling numbers, until the end of the war in early May 1945.

TIGER TURRET

1. Muzzle brake
2. Armoured sleeve
3. Mantlet shield
4. Trunnion
5. Recoil cylinder
6. Articulating binocular sight
7. Breech assembly (vertical sliding breech block)
8. Breech control
9. Commander's cupola
10. Recoil guard
11. Turret ventilator
12. Turret stowage bin
13. Used shell case holder
14. Ammunition stowage (in lockers)
15. Holder for water container
16. Turret base rotary junction
17. Turret traverse hydraulic motor
18. Gunner's seat
19. Co-axial machine-gun firing pedal
20. Gun tube

PRODUCTION-RUN MODIFICATIONS

Like all tanks, the design of the Tiger was regularly modified during the main production run. Indeed, this run can be divided into three main sub-categories – the 'early-', 'mid-', and 'late-' production vehicles, although the transition from one category to another was by no means distinct. The 'early' Tigers – the first 250 tanks – have been described above. The mid-production sequence commenced in late April 1943 with vehicle 251 and continued until chassis 824 in January 1944. All Tigers after vehicle 251 featured the more powerful 694bhp Maybach HL230 engine, as well as an improved transmission, which marginally improved the vehicle's off-road performance. Next, from vehicle 391 in July 1943, Tigers featured a redesigned turret commander's cupola with armoured periscopes instead of visors. From September 1943 onwards (from vehicle 496), the design discontinued the expensive and little-used wading equipment, as an economy measure to boost delivery rates. Tigers completed after this date were also outfitted with Zimmerit paste to protect them from infantry-delivered magnetic mines.

Late-production modifications appeared during the last eight months of Tiger production (January–August 1944) and featured a varying combination of the following features. From January (vehicle 820) onwards, selected vehicles featured the multi-purpose Close Defence Weapon. From this time on, Tigers also began to feature resilient steel-rimmed road wheels in place of the previous rubber-tyred ones. Next, from March (chassis 920 onwards), the turret roof armour was increased from 25mm to 40mm to

Taken in Tunisia in early 1943, this side view of an early Tiger shows it with its wading tube erected. Also visible is the drum-shaped original commander's turret cupola with its vision slits. (TTM 26/H/5)

help protect against plunging fire. Then from around chassis 1100 in April, Tigers featured the monocular TFZ 9c sight in place of the previous binocular TFZ 9b one. Other minor modifications introduced during this period included the addition of stowage brackets on the turret sides to hold five spare track links and the replacement of the two hull roof-mounted headlamps by a single one fitted onto the driver's front plate.

TIGER VARIANTS

The Germans only developed two specialized Tiger tank variants which were both command-tank designs[1]. Henschel produced 89 command Tigers – either the Sdkfz 267 battalion commander's tank or the Sdkfz 268 company commander's vehicle. Both of these were similar to the standard production Tiger tank except for the addition of a powerful radio transmitter. The Sdkfz 267 featured the ultra-long-range Fu-8 30-watt transmitter/medium-range receiver, while the Sdkfz 268 mounted the long-range Fu-7 20-watt transmitter/ultra-short-wave receiver. Both command designs possessed a second aerial to service their additional communication sets, and this enabled friend and foe alike to distinguish these vehicles from standard Tigers. Space was created for these radios by reducing main gun-round stowage to 66 rounds and removing the co-axial machine gun.

Here a mid-production Tiger has been knocked out in Normandy. In this photograph, taken on 26 June 1944 near Rauray, the ripple effect of the Zimmerit paste can be clearly seen, as well as the vertical glacis plate into which are set the driver's visor and the bow machine gun. The feet of a dead soldier can be seen in the left foreground. (IWM B6155)

---

1 The only other significant Tiger variant was the Sturmtiger assault vehicle, developed during 1943–44 to engage heavily fortified enemy bunkers.

This late-production Tiger was captured by British forces in northern Italy early in 1945. Visible is the new-style armoured commander's cupola, with periscopes instead of visors. Obscured by the barrel, this tank probably had the monocular gunner's sight, not the binocular one of the early Tiger. (TTM 2907/C/3)

SPECIFICATIONS: TIGER (VEHICLES 1–250)

General
Production run: August 1942–August 1944 (24 months)
Vehicles produced: 1,349
Combat weight: 55 tons
Crew: five (commander, gunner, loader, driver, radio/bow MG operator)

Dimensions
Overall length: 8.24m
Hull length: 6.20m
Width (with battle tracks): 3.73m
Height: 2.86m

Armour
Hull front: 100mm (at 66–80 degrees)
Hull sides: 60–80mm (at 90 degrees)
Hull rear: 82mm (at 82 degrees)
Hull roof: 25mm (at 90 degrees)
Turret front: 100–120mm (at 80–90 degrees)
Turret sides: 80mm (at 90 degrees)
Turret rear: 80mm (at 90 degrees)
Turret roof: 26mm (at 0–9 degrees)

Armament
Main gun: 1 x 8.8cm KwK 36 L/56

Secondary: 2 x 7.92mm MG 34; 1 co-axial in turret; 1 hull front; 2 x treble smoke dischargers (turret sides)
Main gun rate of fire: 15rpm

Ammunition stowage
Main: 92 rounds (typically 50 per cent PzGr.39 APCBC, 50 per cent Sprgr.L4.5 HE; also few Pzgr.40 APCR, Gr.39HL HEAT)
Secondary: 3,900–5,100 rounds

Communications
Fu-5 Ultra-short-wave transmitter/receiver; intercom

Motive power
Engine: Maybach HL210 P435 21-litre V12-cylinder petrol engine
Power: 642 metric bhp at 3000rpm
Fuel capacity: 534 litres
Power-to-weight ratio: 11.6 HP/ton

Performance
Ground pressure: 1.05kg/cm2
Maximum road speed: 38kph
Maximum cross-country speed: 20kph
Operational range (road): 100km
Operational range (cross-country): 57km
Fuel consumption (road): 5–5.3 litres/km
Fuel consumption (cross-country): 9–9.3 litres/km

FIREFLY

Spurred on by the urgent need to up-gun the Sherman prior to D-Day, the War Office accepted the Firefly for general production in early January 1944. Within days, the War Office placed contracts for the conversion of 2,100 Shermans to the new design in a limited time frame. To meet these contracts, the factories raced with an almost unseemly haste to mount all available 17-pounder guns on any suitable available Sherman chassis. It was not deemed possible to modify the 76mm-gunned Sherman owing to its incompatible turret mantlet design, and so during early 1944 the only suitable Sherman chassis available was the Mark V. As the Firefly production programme unfolded, other compatible Sherman chassis – the Mark I and the I (Hybrid), the latter with a cast-hull front – were used to create the Sherman IC and IC (Hybrid) Firefly.

TIGER/FIREFLY AMMUNITION

AP round: Armour Piercing round. The basic design of a solid tank round with a pointed nose designed to penetrate thick steel armour of enemy tanks through kinetic energy.

APC round: Armour Piercing Capped round. A variant of the AP round that featured a soft metal nose, which gave better penetration performance against sloped armour.

APCBC round: Armour Piercing Capped Ballistic Capped round. A variant of the APC round that featured a brittle cap on top of the soft metal cap, designed to achieve good penetration against sloped armour.

APCR round: Armour Piercing Composite Rigid round. A soft metal round with a small, high-density core; on impact the core is ejected at very high speed from the round, penetrating the target.

APDS round: Armour Piercing Discarding Sabot round. A solid round fired via the medium of a sabot which is squeezed into the rifling and which falls away from the round once fired; enables the round to be fired with greater velocity.

HE round: High Explosive round. A shell filled with explosive filler that explodes on impact to give a large blast area; used to engage 'soft' (that is, unarmoured or lightly armoured) targets such as enemy soldiers, lorries, half-tracks, etc.

HEAT round: High Explosive Anti-Tank round. A conical round filled with explosive filler that penetrates armour through chemical effect (a thin jet of molten-hot metal pierces the plating).

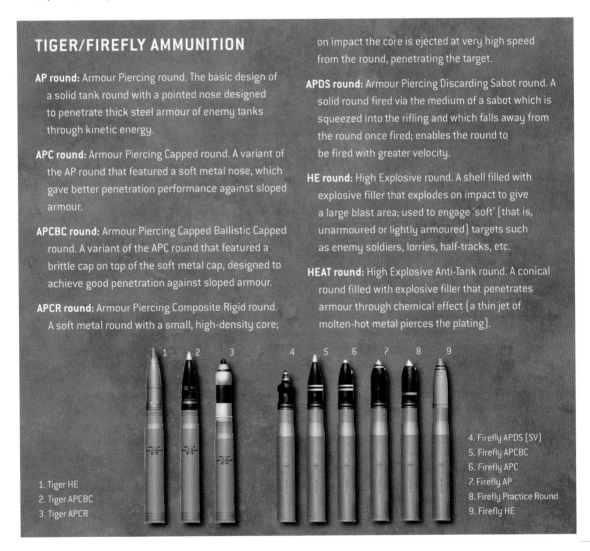

1. Tiger HE
2. Tiger APCBC
3. Tiger APCR

4. Firefly APDS (SV)
5. Firefly APCBC
6. Firefly APC
7. Firefly AP
8. Firefly Practice Round
9. Firefly HE

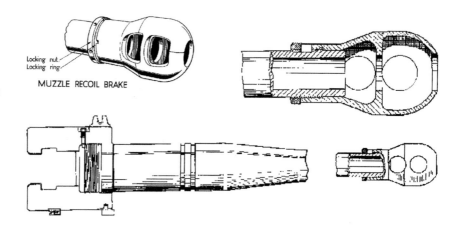

MUZZLE RECOIL BRAKE

Locking nut.
Locking ring.

The War Office later raised its orders to 3,414 Fireflies, of which the factories completed between 2,139 and 2,239 tanks – the documentation remains contradictory – during a 17-month production run from January 1944 to May 1945. This represented an impressive average delivery rate of 126–132 tanks a month, reflecting the fact that the Firefly was an easy-to-accomplish conversion based on an existing chassis and gun. By 31 May 1944, 342 Fireflies had been delivered, the vast majority to Montgomery's 21st Army Group for the D-Day landings. This was sufficient to provide one Firefly per troop, including those squadrons equipped with the Cromwell. Between D-Day and the end of the Normandy campaign in late August 1944, a further 562 Fireflies were produced, sufficient to replace those lost during the campaign. By February 1945, the factories had delivered 2,002 Fireflies, adequate to begin equipping the 21st Army Group with two Fireflies per troop. During spring 1945, however, three factors led to the programme being wound down, with the last tank completed in May: the war in Europe was obviously coming to an end; the Firefly was not required for the Far Eastern theatre, where Japanese tanks lacked the potent guns of the latest Panzers; and the expedient Firefly was being replaced by purpose-designed medium tanks like the A34 Comet. While the Firefly only saw action in British service during the 1944–45 North-West Europe and Italian campaigns, the last confirmed Firefly action occurred during the 1976 clash between Christian Phalangist forces and other Lebanese paramilitaries.

The Firefly was externally similar to the standard Sherman mark upon which it was based. The glaring exception was the much longer barrel of the 17-pounder, which overhung the front of the vehicle; this made the Firefly stand out among standard Shermans. The Germans soon learned to knock out any Fireflies they encountered first before engaging the standard Shermans. For British tank crews who received the tanks at short notice and with little training, this was often an unwelcome surprise. Trooper Joe Ekins of the 1st Northamptonshire Yeomanry (1NY) remained blissfully unaware of this enemy practice until a Panzer knocked out his Firefly on 8 August 1944. In response, the British attempted to disguise the tank by painting the end of the barrel in light colours or even fitting a fake muzzle brake half way along the gun.

The Firefly carried 77 rounds for its main armament, normally a mixture of armour-piercing and High Explosive rounds (HE) just like other tanks. Typically, the

Firefly was supplied with up to five types of ammunition – the Armoured Piercing Capped (APC), APC Ballistic Capped (APCBC), the rare AP Discarding Sabot Super Velocity (APDS-SV), and the two standard Mk I HE rounds. With armour-piercing rounds, the Firefly was a potent tank killer. In terms of textbook penetrative power, the Firefly with the rare APDS round outperformed the Panther, the Tiger and even the new King Tiger which began to reach the battlefields during spring 1944. These Panzers, however, maintained an advantage in accuracy, particularly at longer range. At normal combat ranges, the Firefly's APDS round could penetrate the Tiger's armour from any direction. This was the capability that transformed the Sherman from a satisfactory dual-purpose tank into a lethal tank killer.

The Firefly's major drawback was that a blinding flash, which often threw up a cloud of fumes and dust, emanated from the muzzle brake when the gun was fired; a similar flash, combined with powerful back-blast, also filled the turret. No one warned Trooper Ekins about these occurrences when he fired his first Firefly round in training just prior to D-Day; the shock that ensued was so great that he later reported that he 'nearly jumped out of the tank'. These problems were particularly acute when the Firefly fired HE rounds. Given the velocity at which its rounds were fired, the brief flashes made it difficult for the momentarily blinded Firefly crews to observe the fall of their rounds, which had hit the target before the flash had died down or their sight was restored. The flash also exposed their location to the enemy, forcing tank commanders to regularly move to new firing positions. Despite the technical measures intended to minimize this problem, it was never really solved. As three-quarters of

Trooper G. Aitken of Sussex, New Brunswick, Canada is seen in his Firefly during exercises in Italy. This shot shows the redesigned mantlet required to mount the 17-pounder gun, with the co-axial machine gun visible. Note the unusual twin Vickers K guns mounted on the turret roof. (TTM 2699/E/1)

all tank rounds fired were HE – generally against 'soft' targets like infantry, anti-tank guns and lorries – the Firefly's inadequate HE performance was a serious problem. Given this, British tank squadrons were loath to accept more than two Fireflies per troop, as the standard Shermans were required for their better HE performance.

The Firefly also sported other differences from the typical Sherman tank from which it had been modified. In particular, the standard design needed minor modification to be able to mount the 17-pounder Mark IV gun, including a redesigned turret mantlet. Other observable differences included the large box attached to the turret rear which housed the vehicle's radio and the lack a of hull machine gun. The absence of the latter allowed the crew to be reduced to four, freeing up space in the cramped interior for the large 17-pounder rounds. The combination of the heavier gun and ammunition increased the Firefly's weight to 34.8 tons from the 31.8 tons of the Sherman V. The crew reduction in the Firefly meant that the loader had to double-up as the radio operator. In combat, loaders were so engrossed in loading the tank's main armament that they were hard-pressed to operate the vehicle's communications effectively. This made it more difficult for Fireflies to operate successfully as part of a larger tank unit.

In other respects, however, the expedient Firefly design was all but identical to the standard Sherman. The Firefly featured the same armour as that of the Sherman mark on which it was based; for the Sherman VC, this amounted to sloped frontal armour up to 76mm thick, and 38mm side plates. Thus, at normal combat ranges the Firefly was no more capable of withstanding the lethal fire of the Panzer IV, Panther or Tiger than was the standard Sherman, and if hit it was equally prone to burn. This propensity led understandably scared Firefly crew like Trooper Ekins to bale out as soon as their

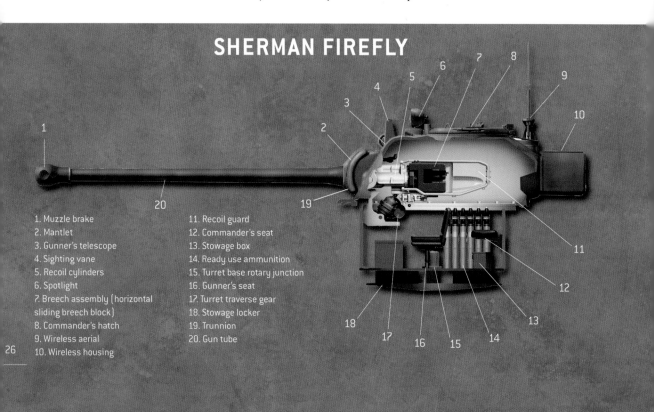

SHERMAN FIREFLY

1. Muzzle brake
2. Mantlet
3. Gunner's telescope
4. Sighting vane
5. Recoil cylinders
6. Spotlight
7. Breech assembly (horizontal sliding breech block)
8. Commander's hatch
9. Wireless aerial
10. Wireless housing
11. Recoil guard
12. Commander's seat
13. Stowage box
14. Ready use ammunition
15. Turret base rotary junction
16. Gunner's seat
17. Turret traverse gear
18. Stowage locker
19. Trunnion
20. Gun tube

tank got hit, lest it 'brewed up'. The VC also had the same Chrysler petrol engine as most Sherman Vs and this – despite the vehicle's slightly increased weight – provided it with the same performance and mobility as that of the standard Sherman.

MAIN-RUN MODIFICATIONS

Due to its relatively brief production run, the Firefly design witnessed fewer modifications than most tanks. Indeed, there was no significant variant to the design. One change that did occur during the production run was that increasing numbers of Sherman I or I (Hybrid) chassis were used for the conversion instead of the Sherman V. Sherman IC Fireflies differed externally to the VC in several ways: ICs had vertical rear plates, not sloped ones; some ICs had an appliqué armour cheek fitted to the right side of the turret front, whereas VCs did not; other ICs had a pistol port in the turret side and open-spoked road wheels, features not generally present on the VC.

SPECIFICATIONS: SHERMAN VC FIREFLY

General
Production run: January 1944–May 1945 (17 months)
Vehicles produced: Between 2,139 and 2,239
Combat weight: 34.8 tons
Crew: Four (commander, gunner, loader/radio operator, driver)

Dimensions
Overall length: 7.82m
Hull length: 6.5m
Width: 2.67m
Height: 2.74m

Armour
Hull front: 51mm (at 45–90 degrees)
Hull sides: 38mm (at 90 degrees)
Hull rear: 38mm (at 70–90 degrees)
Hull roof: 25mm (at 0 degrees)
Turret front: 38–76mm (at 85–90 degrees)
Turret sides: 51mm (at 85 degrees)
Turret rear: 64mm (at 90 degrees)
Turret roof: 25mm (at 0 degrees)

Armament
Main gun: 1 x 17-pounder (76.2mm, 3in) ROQF Mk IV or Mk VII

Secondary: 1 x 0.3 calibre co-axial M1919A4 machine gun
Main gun rate of fire: 10rpm

Ammunition stowage
Main: 77 rounds (typically 50 per cent APCBC/APDS, 50 per cent HE)
Secondary: 5,000 rounds

Communications
No. 19 Set transmitter/receiver

Motive power
Engine: Chrysler Multibank A57 30-cylinder petrol engine
Power: 443 metric bhp at 2,850rpm
Fuel capacity: 604 litres
Power-to-weight ratio: 12.9HP/ton

Performance
Ground pressure: 0.92kg/cm2
Maximum road speed: 36kph
Maximum cross-country speed: 17kph
Operational range (road): 201km
Operational range (cross-country): 145km
Fuel consumption (road): 3 litres/km
Fuel consumption (cross-country): 4.2 litres/km

A rare view of a Sherman IC (Hybrid) Firefly with cast-hull front. This view also shows nicely the fake muzzle brake located half-way down the barrel and the disruptive camouflage scheme used to disguise the tank's tell-tale longer barrel. (PA-115712)

Other minor modifications introduced during the production run reflected attempts to reduce the flash emitted when the gun was fired and to improve its accuracy when firing APDS. Later Fireflies incorporated a slightly modified muzzle brake with an altered internal bore that enabled the tank to fire APDS rounds more accurately at longer ranges; REME teams carried out this modification on tanks already in theatre. Another such development was the introduction of improved HE rounds like the Mk.IIT Reduced Charge shell that reduced the round's muzzle velocity and thus the amount of blast created. The only other significant change made during the Firefly production run was the moving of the gun's travel rest – which was needed to protect the long barrel when the tank was being transported – from the centre of the rear hull deck to the left side. This modification was designed to make it easier for the driver to escape quickly from the tank if it had started to burn after receiving an enemy hit.

THE STRATEGIC SITUATION

During spring 1944, the forces of General Bernard Montgomery's British 21st Army Group trained relentlessly for the Allied D-Day landings on the coast of German-occupied Normandy, finally initiated on 6 June. Both sides knew that the outcome of these landings – and the ensuing battle for Normandy – held monumental significance for the course of the war. It was not surprising, therefore, that during this period the first Sherman Fireflies to be completed were rushed to the British and Canadian armoured units then finalizing their preparations for D-Day. These units, which included the 1st Northamptonshire Yeomanry (1NY), held high hopes that the Firefly would enable them to defeat the enemy's most potent tanks including the Tiger. Senior German commanders in turn held equally high expectations for what the Tiger would contribute to the imminent struggle, hoping that it would spearhead the defensive and the counter-offensive actions required to halt and even reverse the Allied invasion. This was a particularly tall order, as the German Army in the West (Westheer) typically deployed fewer than 80 operational Tigers. Nevertheless, battlefield events within a week of the landings showed that these grandiose German expectations were not unrealistic. On 13 June, in a famous incident, a few Tigers led by Michael Wittmann mauled the British armoured brigade that had thrust audaciously south to Villers Bocage.

But such isolated examples of successful German counter-attacks were not sufficient to stop the gradual expansion of the Allied beachhead in Normandy. However, the Tiger's defensive prowess did help the Germans slow the Allied advance to a crawl, frustrating Montgomery's plan to create a sizable lodgement area bordered by the

Loire and Seine Rivers by early September. By mid-July the Tiger's capabilities had helped turn the Normandy campaign into a bloody attritional war of matériel. These hard-fought battles again demonstrated the vulnerability of the Sherman (and thus the Firefly) to German tank fire, as well as the Tiger's virtual invulnerability to 75mm-gunned Sherman fire. On 18 July, during Operation *Goodwood*, for example, 11th Armoured Division lost 21 of its 34 Fireflies to enemy tank and anti-tank fire in just one day. Despite such setbacks, on numerous occasions Sherman and Firefly crews bravely engaged Tigers, with many of them paying the ultimate price for their gallantry. An unofficial dictum soon sprung up in British armoured units – if a Tiger appeared, send out a troop of four Shermans (with its single Firefly) to destroy the Panzer, and only expect one to come home. Understandably, after such painful combat experiences some Allied tank crews became so concerned about the Tiger's capabilities that 'Tiger-phobia' became evident. One brigadier recorded an extreme manifestation of this phobia, when a solitary German Tiger 'fired for one hour ... [and] then drove off unmolested ... [because] not one tank went out to engage it'.

Despite the disproportionate damage done by the few Tigers deployed in Normandy, the combination of Allied numerical superiority, offensive determination and the Firefly's lethal gun gradually wore down the Westheer's powers of resistance while Allied tank crews' confidence increased. For the bitter armoured battles waged in Normandy showed that the Firefly's potent 17-pounder gun could indeed take out

The strategic situation, 7 August 1944

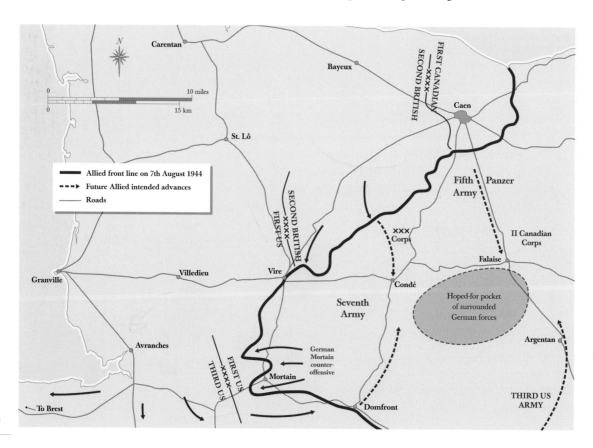

even the much-feared Tiger. During a 96-hour period of the late-June *Epsom* offensive, British 11th Armoured Division Fireflies knocked out or disabled five Tigers in a series of bitter encounters. Aided by the Firefly's firepower, the repeated Allied attacks finally bore fruit in late July when Lt-Gen Bradley's First US Army *Cobra* offensive broke through the German front around St-Lô. Just prior to this Montgomery's *Goodwood* offensive had advanced the Anglo-Canadian front to the Bourguébus Ridge, from where the *Totalize* offensive commenced on 7–8 August. Between 31 July and 6 August, American forces – having passed the bottom corner of the Cotentin peninsula and with the German line shattered – raced west into Brittany, south towards the Loire and east towards the Seine.

Hitler now blundered strategically by ordering the Westheer to counter-attack the narrow corridor located behind the American breakout. Consequently, during 6–7 August, German armour attacked west towards Mortain. This ill-advised attack predictably failed and in so doing sucked German forces further west, pulling them deeper into a large encirclement that was beginning to form in the Mortain–Argentan area. For by 8 August – by which time *Totalize* had commenced – American forces had raced south-east to capture Le Mans, deep into the German rear. Meanwhile, the western part of the Allied front, manned by Montgomery's two Anglo-Canadian armies, had remained relatively static, from the coast to the Bourguébus Ridge and thence south-west to Vire, where the American sector began. By 8 August, therefore,

Taken from a nearby building, this top view shows two Canadian Fireflies moving through the streets of Douvres-la-Deliverande on 8 June 1944. The image again reveals the extent to which the 17-pounder gun overhung the front of the tank. (IWM B568)

it now seemed possible that if the infant *Totalize* offensive could secure Falaise, its forces might then be able to link up around Argentan with the north-westerly American advance beyond Le Mans. In so doing, the Allies would have encircled substantial German forces in a giant pocket.

OPERATION *TOTALIZE*

Crusader anti-aircraft tanks, equipped with 20mm Oerlikon cannon, of the 1st Polish Armoured Division, move forward during 7 August in preparation for the start of Operation *Totalize* at 2330 hours that night. (PA-116249)

Lt-Gen Guy Simonds's II Canadian Corps *Totalize* offensive aimed to advance 24km south from the Bourguébus Ridge to secure the high ground that dominated the town of Falaise. The offensive had originally been intended to aid the advance of British forces located further west. By the time it was launched on the night of 7–8 August, however, *Totalize* had acquired greater strategic significance, as the precursor to the Allies being able to close the Falaise pocket, which had developed in the Falaise–Argentan area. First Canadian Army commander General Crerar had stated his expectation that *Totalize* would play a pivotal role in the campaign, by making 'the 8th August 1944 an even blacker day for the German Armies than is recorded against that same date twenty-six years ago' during the Great War battle at Amiens.

Simonds's five divisions and two independent brigades would attack the defences manned by the 89th Infantry Division (part of I SS Panzer Corps), while the 12th SS Panzer Division *Hitlerjugend* held reserve positions further south. During the offensive's first phase, two infantry divisions would attack south astride the main Caen–Falaise road in an initial surprise night break-in operation, aided by night-time heavy bombers. Seven mobile columns – formed of tanks and infantry embussed in armoured vehicles – would spearhead the attack by audaciously infiltrating between the forward defensive localities (FDLs) to seize objectives deep in the German rear. Simultaneously, infantry would attack the FDLs the columns had bypassed.

Aided by surprise, during the night of 7–8 August this first phase of *Totalize* went extremely well. By mid-morning on the 8th, Simonds's forces had secured a 6km-deep rupture of the German front. According to the commander of the *Hitlerjugend* – SS-Oberführer (Senior Colonel) Kurt Meyer – this advance had smashed the 89th Division, thus creating a yawning gap in the German front that remained undefended and unoccupied. Meyer commanded a unique German division. The *Hitlerjugend* had been raised during spring 1943 as part of Germany's general mobilization towards total war that followed in the wake of the disaster at Stalingrad. The elite division mainly comprised 16- and 17-year-olds from the Hitler Youth movement who, despite being too young to join the armed forces, had nevertheless volunteered to enlist in this unique

The break-in phase of Operation *Totalize*.

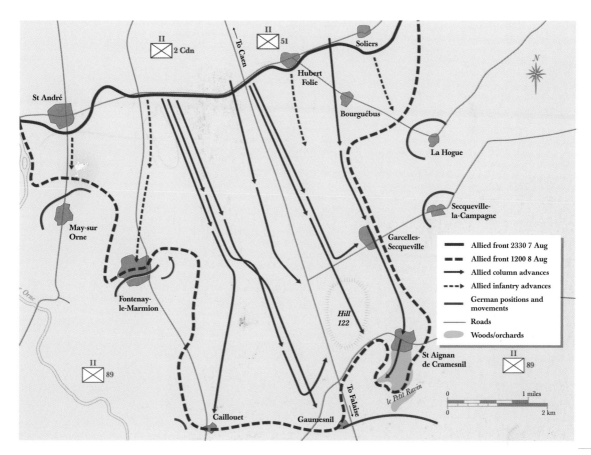

33

The key Allied players in Operation *Totalize*; the front row from left to right: First Canadian Army commander General Crerar; the British CIGS Alan Brooke; II Canadian Corps commander Guy Simonds; and 21st Army Group commander Bernard Montgomery. Simonds had a reputation as a ruthless and determined commander who took it badly when his subordinates failed to deliver the success he expected – rightly or not – from them. *Totalize* showed that Simonds's operational planning was sophisticated, but some of those subordinates tasked with executing his grandiose plans felt that Simonds had forgotten the fact that for centuries the principle of 'simplicity' had been a well-proven maxim of war. (Barney J. Gloster/PA-143952)

SS division. Many fought with great determination in Normandy, but the division's battlefield performance was stained by the war crimes its personnel committed in murdering dozens of Allied prisoners of war.

During the late morning of 8 August, Simonds's offensive began its second phase – the daytime break-in operation directed against the enemy's reserve defence line located between Bretteville and St-Sylvain. His two reserve armoured divisions moved south of Caen, ready to move up to the front to spearhead this assault. Erroneously believing this second German position to be a formidable one, Simonds had arranged that a second bombing strike should smash the enemy line shortly after noon. That morning 681 American B-17 Flying Fortresses droned their way south from England towards the Falaise plain, striking six German targets between 1226 and 1355 hours. The late morning of 8 August thus witnessed a largely unavoidable lull in the Allied advance as Simonds's forces readied themselves for the second phase while waiting for the bombers to arrive. Perhaps rather unfairly, Kurt Meyer lambasted the German tactics during this period since they 'transferred the initiative from … leading combat elements to timetable acrobats [back] at Headquarters'. Unfortunately for the Allies, during this lull the enemy began recovering from the shock inflicted upon them by the successful night attack. Orchestrated by Meyer, the Germans now launched counter-measures against the Allied penetration.

Around 1135 hours that morning, Meyer was being driven north to Cintheaux when he encountered German infantrymen retreating south in disorder. Meyer stood 'alone in the middle of the road … armed with just a carbine' and through

much bravado rallied the fleeing troops. Subsequently, Meyer met up with SS-Sturmbannführer (Major) Hans Waldmüller and the two officers drove up onto the gentle rise situated north-east of Gaumesnil to reconnoitre the front. Shortly before noon, from the vantage point of a barn, the two officers observed the spearheads of Simonds's two armoured divisions formed up behind the front apparently ready to strike south. The two officers were hardened veterans, but this display of Allied offensive strength nevertheless took their breath away.

Meyer knew that if this armour struck south it would smash through the as-yet only thinly held German reserve line; if this transpired, 'nothing could have prevented the Canadians from taking Falaise that evening'. Meyer knew instinctively what such a crisis demanded – whatever meagre forces were immediately available to him must act immediately to prevent the Allied armour thrusting south. The odds could not have been higher, for with Falaise lost, an entire German army might well be subsequently encircled in the Domfront–Falaise–Argentan area. After such a disaster, the German defence of Normandy would collapse and the entire course of the war could be decided. Meyer ordered that all *Hitlerjugend* units in the vicinity should counter-attack north at 1230 hours. While this scratch force was woefully weak, it did nonetheless contain four or five of Wittmann's powerful Tigers, and it was upon these tanks that Meyer placed most of his slim hopes for success.

Meyer had unwittingly now initiated the series of events that would bring to a dramatic conclusion the epic struggle of Firefly and Tiger in Normandy. Would the awesome firepower and massive armour of a handful of Wittmann's Tigers prove

The initial night-time break-in phase of Operation *Totalize* secured significant success. Here a Sherman has been knocked out during the attack that secured May-sur-Orne on the afternoon of 8 August. (Ken Bell/PA-131352)

PANZER ACE MICHAEL WITTMANN

Wittmann's Gunner:
   'They are behaving as if they'd won the war already.'
Michael Wittmann:
   'We're going to prove them wrong.'
(Villers Bocage, Normandy, 13 June 1944).

Born a farmer's son on 22 April 1914, Michael Wittmann rose to become one of Germany's leading Tiger tank aces. After service in the German Army as a private during 1934–36, Wittmann enlisted in the elite *Leibstandarte SS Adolf Hitler*. After service in the 1939 Polish campaign, Wittmann led a StuG III assault gun platoon during the spring 1940 Balkan war. Next, he participated in the invasion of the Soviet Union, during which he received the Iron Cross First Class and promotion to SS-Oberscharführer (Sergeant) for his outstanding performance as a destroyer of Soviet tanks. After officer training, SS-Untersturmführer (Second Lieutenant) Wittmann rejoined the *Leibstandarte* in December 1942. While serving with the division's Tiger-equipped 13th Heavy Company, he again performed well during the July 1943 Battle of Kursk, thanks to his careful planning of actions and the 'unshakable calm' he maintained during combat. This company then formed the nucleus of the newly raised 101st SS Heavy Tank Battalion, with which Wittmann continued to serve until his death on 8 August 1944. During January 1944, the newly promoted SS-Obersturmführer (Lieutenant) Wittmann received the Knight's Cross, and then the Oakleaves to this coveted award, for his tally of over 90 enemy kills. By the time he assumed command of the 101st Battalion's 2nd Company in March, Wittmann had also married Hildegard Burmester. Goebbel's propaganda machine now seized upon Wittmann's exploits and transformed this modest yet determined officer into a national hero.

   On 13 June 1944, Wittmann joined combat in Normandy with the 101st Battalion. That day his Tigers inflicted a bloody repulse on the British 7th Armoured Division at Villers Bocage. Wittmann's Tiger was on reconnaissance when he observed the spearhead tanks of the British 22nd Armoured Brigade advancing through the hazy daylight near Villers Bocage. Wittmann's Tiger moved west behind the column while four other Tigers moved east to attack its spearhead.

Image courtesy of Bundesarchiv

Catching the column by surprise, the Tigers poured fire into it, leaving around 20 enemy vehicles burning furiously.

   So far the Tigers had triumphed, but the second half of the action did not go as well for them. By the time that Wittmann, possibly supported by two other Tigers, headed west into Villers Bocage, the 22nd Brigade had established an effective defensive position. One Sherman Firefly, three Churchill tanks and a 6-pounder anti-tank gun had deployed in the town's side-streets, ready to ambush the Tigers with close-range fire against their more vulnerable side armour. As the Panzers moved through the main street, the anti-tank gun engaged and disabled Wittmann's Tiger, forcing the crew to flee on foot. Ultimately that day the Germans lost at least four Tigers in the actions that raged all day around Villers Bocage, while the Allies lost at least 10 tanks and around 20 other vehicles. With this feat behind him, Wittmann served in the bitter defensive stands the Germans enacted in and around Caen during July. Yet on 8 August – by which time the now SS-Hauptsturmführer (Captain) Wittmann had claimed 139 combat kills – the Panzer ace met a warrior's end during a desperate counter-attack launched against numerically superior Allied forces.

sufficient to defy the massive odds stacked against them? Could Wittmann's desperate charge north towards the Allied lines prevent the seemingly imminent collapse of the German front north of Falaise? Or would the proven 'Tiger-killing' capabilities of Simonds's Fireflies prove sufficient to thwart Meyer's audacious attempt to snatch victory out of the jaws of defeat? This was the epic contest between Firefly and Tiger about to be waged across the battlefields of Europe.

Senior *Hitlerjugend* officers discuss the battlefield situation on 9 June 1944; from right to left: the then commander of SS Panzer-grenadier Regiment 25, Kurt Meyer; the then divisional commander Fritz Witt; and the leader of the division's Panzer regiment, Max Wünnsche. When Witt was killed by Allied naval gunfire on 12 June, Meyer took command of the *Hitlerjugend* and directed the fanatical resistance the division offered during the Normandy campaign. A ruthless commander, Meyer was later convicted by an Allied military court of war crimes, after evidence was discovered that indicated that *Hitlerjugend* personnel had executed as many as 155 Canadian prisoners of war during early June 1944. (Budesarchiv 146/88/28/259)

THE COMBATANTS

To be able to fully understand the realities of this clash of rival armour that occurred in Normandy during mid-1944, one has to appreciate the realities of tank combat at the time, including an understanding of the way in which Firefly and Tiger crews were trained, how these tanks were organized into combat units and what daily life was like for Tiger and Firefly crews both in combat and in the quieter periods in between actions.

Throughout the 1939–45 war, Panzer troops represented an elite arm that spearheaded German military operations. The Panzer arm received the best personnel, hand-picked for their outstanding leadership and technical capabilities. These personnel were exposed to extensive specialized training to produce some of the finest tank crews of the war. Of course, as the war progressed the overall quality of Panzer troops inevitably declined as the standard of available German personnel and training declined. Nevertheless they remained an elite until the German surrender, and the small number of Tiger tank crews that existed represented an elite within this elite.

TRAINING

All recruits for the German Army and Waffen-SS began their military service with a programme of basic training as infantrymen. Only when this was completed would the recruits apply to undertake further training – either as other ranks or as aspirant officers – with the specialized branch of their choice – Panzer troops, mountain troops, engineers, signallers, etc. Only a proportion of those recruits and aspirant officers who put themselves forward for the popular branch of the Panzer forces were accepted for specialized training. The Panzer arm invariably only selected those recruits who had excelled in basic training. To fill the role of tank commander, the branch sought to recruit exceptional leaders who could swiftly size up a complex tactical situation and execute a timely decision based upon this appraisal. The Panzer branch also required experienced mechanics and highly skilled technicians to serve as tank drivers, gunners and wireless operators. The tank loader was probably the least technically qualified member of the crew – but this physically demanding role was just as vital to the performance of the tank as the others. In practice, some Tiger commander's roles were filled by accomplished former gunners or drivers who had completed specialist refresher courses. It was less common for a loader to be promoted to command a tank, although this is precisely what occurred with Otto Carius, who went on to become one of Germany's leading Tiger aces.

Specialized Panzer arm training was undertaken at one of the many dedicated armoured training schools located within the Reich. Personnel received extensive training in the tank-crew role for which they had been selected, as well as more superficial training in the other crew roles. Such training also sought to instil within a particular tank crew a smooth and efficient interaction between the various team members. Nowhere was this interaction more crucial than in the interplay between commander, gunner and loader in the drills performed for engaging enemy tanks. The crews honed these skills by regularly conducting live firing on the ranges and proving grounds located within the Reich; around 20 of the earliest Tigers had been allocated to the training schools for this purpose.

A group of Panzer crewmen from the Leibstandarte SS Adolf Hitler. They have elected to wear the full two-piece camouflaged version of the Panzer uniform. This shot can be considered typical of the appearance of an SS tank crew from 1943 through to the end of the war. (Schumann)

The basic German tank engagement drill ran as follows. Once a tank commander had spotted an enemy tank, he would indicate the bearing and order the crew to engage it. If necessary, the driver would move the Tiger to a better firing position. Then, looking through his superb Zeiss gunsight, the gunner would calculate the range and lay the main gun onto the target, compensating for expected trajectory disturbances caused by strong cross-winds or the spinning of the round in flight. In the meantime, the loader had man-handled a long Tiger APCBC round into the gun's breech mechanism. Unless the target was at close range, most first anti-tank shots from a Tiger were regarded merely as an acquisition shot, expected to be more likely to land near the target rather than hit it. The gunner then corrected the range (by bracketing the range up or down in increments of 50m–200m), and/or the direction (by aiming off the target to allow for wind and round deflection in flight). With these compensations made, the crew then fired a second round. This shot – termed firing for effect – was expected to hit (and hopefully destroy) the target. German training taught crews to expect to be the first tank to hit an enemy target, rather than to be the first tank to fire in any given engagement.

TIGERFIBEL – THE TANK GUIDE FOR TIGER CREWS

The principal doctrinal guide for Tiger crews was the Tiger Primer, which was accepted as Field Service Regulation D656/27 by Inspector-General of Panzer Troops Col-Gen Heinz Guderian on 1 August 1943. The Primer was unlike other German service regulations, which were famed for their dry technical prose. Instead the Primer was an informal and humorous practical guide to the use of the Tiger in combat. The book used amusing rhymes, mottoes, jokes and cartoons to convey the wealth of valuable common-sense ideas it contained within its covers. The guide went through the duties of each crewman in turn, presenting regulations, useful practices and the 'tricks of the trade'. It implored gunners to 'think before you shoot' because 'for each round that you fire, your father has paid 100RM in taxes [and] your mother has worked a week in the factory'. The Primer likened effective driving of the Tiger to a Viennese waltz, and admonished drivers from crashing through buildings, as the dust clogged the air filters and radiator, causing the engine to overheat. The tactical discussion of how to engage enemy tanks presented a list of anti-heroes that featured characters such as Generals Lee and Sherman, as well as King Voroshilov I.

TIGER ACE OTTO CARIUS

One of the leading exponents of the art of effective combat with the Tiger was Lieutenant Otto Carius, who as reward for his total of over 150 enemy 'kills' received the Oakleaves to the coveted Knight's Cross. Born on 27 May 1922 at Zweibrücken, Carius finally managed to voluntarily join the German Army in May 1940, having been previously turned down twice on the grounds that he was underweight. After basic training as an infantryman, Carius put his name forward for the much sought-after armoured forces. Subsequently, he served as a loader in a Panzer 38(t) of the 1st company of the 21st Panzer Regiment. Immediately on completing its training, the German High Command committed this regiment, as part of its parent formation 20th Panzer Division, to Operation *Barbarossa* – the 1941 invasion of the Soviet Union. During the *Barbarossa* campaign, the now Sergeant Carius was wounded in action, for which he was awarded the Wound Badge in Black. In late 1942 Carius underwent officer training before being posted to the 502nd Heavy Tank Battalion in April 1943. As a commander of a Tiger in the battalion's second company, Carius served during 1943–44 on the northern sector of the Eastern Front. It was during these battles, that Carius's mastery of the Tiger tank became evident. On 22 July 1944, Carius's Tiger, plus another Tiger, launched a bold counter-attack on a Soviet armoured spearhead that had advanced to the village of Malinava, north of Daugavpils in Latvia. Catching the enemy by surprise, the accurate fire of Carius's Tiger dispatched some 16 T-34s and one new JS heavy tank in a matter of 20 minutes. This stunning success ranks alongside Michael Wittmann's June 1944 victory at Villers Bocage as probably the most impressive Tiger action of the entire war.

In August 1944, Carius took command of the 2nd Company of the newly forming 512th Heavy Anti-Tank Battalion, which was to be equipped with the monstrous 65-ton *Jagdtiger* tank destroyer. By early 1945, this unit was still in training with its new vehicles at Döllersheim near Vienna, as the Western Allies successfully advanced towards the Rhine. On 8 March 1945, the desperate German High Command felt compelled to commit the part-trained battalion to action on the Western Front near Siegburg. Despite Carius's tactical abilities, his 2nd Company could not prevent the American forces from overwhelming the flimsy German defensive screen thrown up along the eastern bank of the Rhine. Indeed, by mid-April, the battalion had been surrounded – along with most of Army Group B – in the Ruhr. Carius's unit surrendered to American forces alongside some 300,000 other German troops. Whether the mighty *Jagdtiger* would have withstood the Firefly's potent gun remains uncertain, as Carius's company only saw service against the Americans, who did not generally used 17-pounder-equipped Shermans. After his release from American captivity, Carius went on to run a pharmacy named, rather appositely, *Der Tiger Apotheke*, and as of 2006 Carius was still active at the ripe old age of 84. Today he is still widely considered as one of the greatest tank commanders of the war.

In each military district the Commander of Panzer Troops controlled at least one school along with a host of Panzer training units, where the basic gunnery training took place. In addition to these basic gunnery drills, the training done at these schools covered the whole gamut of professional knowledge. The recruits received instruction and practical exercises in the science of ballistics, in the various drills associated with vehicle maintenance and effective use of the tank's communications devices. In addition, personnel received instruction in combat tactics and the tactics of Tiger tanks cooperating with other combat arms, notably the Panzergrenadiers, the anti-tank troops and the artillery. This all-arms capability was tested exhaustively during the final phases of specialized training, when various tank crews practised operating as coherent tactical units – troops or companies– in a series of exacting field exercises. Personnel also participated in such exercises if they joined a Panzer regiment that was working-up, re-building or re-equipping. Such exercises took place at armoured manoeuvre areas, like that at Putlos, in northern Germany, and Senne, near Paderborn. Armoured demonstration units were often attached to these grounds, where the experienced, high-calibre combat veterans employed in such units demonstrated the correct tactics to be employed by a Tiger unit. The calibre of these instructors is attested to by the fact that in July 1944, SS Tiger ace Michael Wittmann was offered a place at such a school; he turned the posting down on the grounds that his skills were desperately needed at the front. The importance the German military attached to this training is indicated by the fact that even in those last desperate weeks of the war, they largely resisted the powerful temptation of throwing half-trained Panzer units into the many breaches that had emerged in the German line.

The training regime of Firefly crews bore much resemblance, in a general sense, to that of Tiger crews. After basic training, those selected for service in the Royal Armoured Corps would join one of the latter's training regiments. Here recruits learned their specialist trade – commander, driver, wireless operator and loader. With a crew of just four – the Firefly had no hull machine-gun or wireless operator (the latter task was undertaken by the loader) – specialist training was by necessity modified from that for the standard Sherman. In addition, the often laborious general tank maintenance and field-care work done by five had to be done by just four individuals. In addition to their specialist roles, RAC personnel also received instruction and training in the other roles of a tank crew. One RAC private, for example, recalled this approach at the 51st RAC Training Regiment in Yorkshire. In the morning the recruits received instruction in engine maintenance. Every other afternoon a group of three went off in an Austin Seven car to learn the art of navigating a vehicle by map and by communicating with higher headquarters; the individual who was the map reader on the first excursion would drive during the next outing, before acting as wireless operator on the third trip.

Like their German counterparts, British Army tank recruiting also looked for tank commanders who could make good split-second decisions. Personally brave to observe out of the cupola while in action, a good commander had to respond instantly to the flash of an enemy round being fired towards his tank – this round would invariably hit the tank before the sound of it being fired reached the intended tank due to the speed at which it travelled. The British Army also looked to recruit as drivers men who combined good mechanical skills with steely imperturbability; after all, drivers were the only members of a tank crew who could see a lot of what was happening, yet had to remain passive as the commander, gunner and loader slogged it out with the enemy. Tank drivers generally began their training on motor vehicles and progressed to out-of-date armoured vehicles before commencing training in the type of tank they were to drive when they got posted to their slated operational unit. Moreover, drivers of Fireflies – like those of Tigers – had to be trained to drive with special attention to the long barrel overhang, otherwise a tank descending a bank or traversing in a narrow street could get the gun stuck. While embarrassing on manoeuvres, making such an error in action could be fatal.

Towards the end of their training, the recruits found themselves receiving increasing amounts of instruction and undertaking exercises in unit tactics as well as participating in live-firing practice on the ranges. The personnel were trained in how to operate their individual vehicles as part of a wider tactical entity and introduced to the tactical realities of combat that now existed during this middle phase of the war. Operating as part of a Sherman unit was particularly difficult because the hard-pressed loader had to perform the key duty of wireless operator as well, which in part accounts for tank troop leaders preferring to operate from standard 75mm and 76mm gunned Shermans rather than Fireflies.

Initially, the training of Firefly crews to an adequate standard proved problematic because British units only received Fireflies a few weeks prior to D-Day. Trooper Ekins of the 1NY, for example, got only one day on the firing ranges at Linney Head, during which he fired just five rounds. To enable Firefly crew to operate their tanks effectively, this training had to drill them in the effective handling of much heavier rounds within the confined Sherman turret. This training also drilled them in how to combat the effects of the back-blast and flash that erupted when the gun was fired. This led Firefly crews to practise the execution of a more complicated firing drill than was usual with the standard 75mm-gunned Sherman; this necessary drill inevitably slowed the rate of fire that could be obtained from the Firefly's gun. First, the commander gave the order to engage a target. Next, the loader/radio operator – usually a physically strong individual – cradled the heavy and long round in both hands and edged it into the breech. The loader then tapped the commander on the legs to signal that the gun was loaded. Meanwhile, the gunner had acquired the target and the commander warned the crew that the gun was about to be fired with a '3-2-1-fire!' This gave the crew sufficient time to close their eyes, open their mouths and hold their hands over their earphones – all required to withstand the powerful shockwave and flash produced when the gun was fired. Looking out, the commander would attempt to spot the fall of the shot and size up the tactical situation before initiating the drill all over again if need be.

British and Canadian tank training also attached more importance to multi-role training than the Germans. In large part this was due to the long time – sometimes over two years – that some tank units spent in the UK training for D-Day. Thus, through a series of periodic training courses held during the war, many Allied tank crewmen became skilled in several roles. Trooper Ekins received extensive training in the roles of gunner, driver and wireless operator, although not on the Firefly. That many Allied tank crew possessed multiple professional skills meant that crew could be swiftly moved from role to role within the same tank or between tanks, to replace the inevitable casualties that occurred in combat. However, in comparison to battle-hardened German veterans, many Allied crews lacked real combat experience. Whatever the differences, British and German training ensured that when the Firefly clashed with the Tiger in Normandy, these actions were fought by crews that were as well-prepared as possible considering the circumstances.

UNIT ORGANIZATION

During the 1944 Normandy campaign, each British/Canadian Sherman-equipped armoured regiment theoretically fielded 59 Sherman tanks. The regiment fielded three squadrons (usually designated 'A', 'B' and 'C') each with 19 Shermans, plus a Regimental HQ troop of two Shermans. Each armoured squadron comprised four troops, which each fielded four Shermans, plus a headquarters troop of three Shermans. In Normandy, there were sufficient Fireflies to equip just one vehicle per standard troop of four. Thus, in theory, each full-strength squadron should have possessed four Fireflies and 13 Shermans, and thus a regiment ought to have 12 Fireflies and 47 standard Shermans. One Firefly also featured in each troop of armoured regiments equipped with the Cromwell cruiser tank. A British/Canadian armoured brigade fielded three regiments, and thus had a maximum strength of 36 Fireflies and around 145 other tanks. Four British armoured brigades existed in Normandy as independent formations, while an additional three served in the three British armoured divisions employed in Normandy. In addition, just prior to and during the Normandy campaign, each armoured division's reconnaissance regiment was re-equipped with Shermans (and thus Fireflies), turning into defacto fourth armoured regiment.

A Firefly crew have removed their tank's engine so that they can undertake major preventative maintenance on it. (IWM B8893)

The precise role that the Firefly played within the troop varied to a degree between units. Many regiments gave command of a Firefly to an experienced NCO. This was the scheme employed by the 1NY in early August 1944, with all but three of its 12 Fireflies commanded by sergeants and the remainder by corporals. Fireflies tended not to be used as the troop commander's vehicle, however, because the smaller crew of four struggled to undertake the additional task associated with command of a tank troop.

During 1943–45, the principal German unit that deployed Tiger tanks was the heavy tank battalion. The German Army ultimately raised ten such battalions and the Waffen-SS three. When at full strength, these battalions each fielded 45 Tigers – organized in three companies of 14 tanks, plus three Tigers in the headquarters. Each company fielded three troops of four tanks, plus two in the company headquarters. Two other types of German unit also fielded Tigers. The three premier SS divisions and one select army division each possessed a single heavy Panzer company during some phases of the war. Finally, there were also four army heavy radio-controlled tank companies, in which Tigers operated alongside remote-controlled demolition vehicles. The Westheer only ever deployed one army and two SS Tiger battalions, plus one Tiger company, to the Normandy front line.

DAILY LIFE IN THE TIGER AND FIREFLY

Daily life for the crew of a Tiger or a Firefly was essentially similar to that of any tank crew in World War II. The tanker's world was a small one. The nucleus of his existence was the vehicle's crew – a small group of four or five individuals. With so much of the tanker's life spent in a cramped metal container, and with the shared experiences of mortal danger and adrenalin rush of combat, tank crews soon became

The entire crew of Corporal Snowden's 75mm-gunned Sherman of No. 3 Troop, 'C' Squadron, 1NY, use the long barrel rod to clean the gun rifling of any impurities that could impair the accuracy of the weapon. This demanding chore had to be carried out on a daily basis. (IWM B8795)

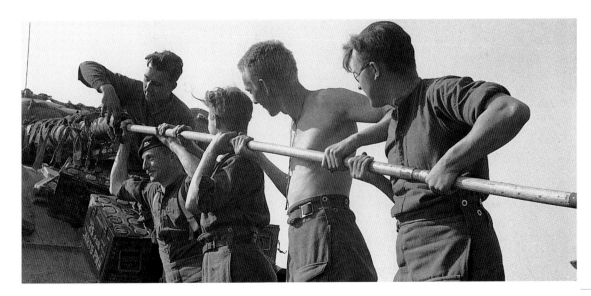

tightly knit cohesive communities. Most individual tank commanders after all were 'only' NCOs – only troop or larger unit commanders were officers. Given the hierarchical nature of military organizations a surprisingly egalitarian atmosphere often emerged within a tank. Trooper Ekins, for example, recalled that military discipline was all but non-existent in his tank. The crew called the NCO commander 'Hog' and referred to one another by their first names. Many decisions taken outside of the heat of battle, Ekins recalled, were formed through democratic consensus.

That is not to say that the commander, whatever his rank, was not the centre of the crew's world, for the crew's fate rested upon the speed of the commander's reactions and the correctness of his decisions. Yet, beyond this, the survival of the crew also depended on how well each crewman performed his own specialized role. No matter how quickly a keen-eyed commander spotted an enemy tank and ordered it to be engaged, the ability of the tank to hit its opponent first rested on the driving skills of the driver, the strength and dexterity of the loader and the marksmanship of the gunner; even the wireless operator played a part if supporting vehicles were required on the scene. Therefore, a particularly strong sense of functional interdependence developed within a tank crew who were only as strong as the weakest man amongst them. Tank crews also developed a very personal relationship with their vehicle, in which they spent so much time. Crews soon grew accustomed to the nuances of the rumblings of the engine and the chink of changing gears. After all, their lives depended on such things working effectively. To many crews, therefore, the tank itself became a living thing that represented the fifth (in a Firefly) or sixth (in a Tiger) member of the crew. Often – and one might hypothesize all sorts of reasons for this – the tank was the only female in the group, identified with popular names such as 'Betty' and 'Mavis', or 'Irma' and 'Brunhilde'.

Many experienced tank commanders (like Wittman and Sergeant Gordon) bravely eschewed the safety of going into action with the cupola hatches closed in order to gain that vital advantage of good observation of the battlefield – itself often the difference between survival and death. Here Sergeant S. Driver, MM, looks out from the open cupola of his 13th/18th Hussars' Firefly in southern England on 30 May 1944. (IWM H38969)

Like most tankers, Firefly and Tiger crews spent much of their time out of combat, engaged in routine maintenance work. This was particularly true of the Tiger, which was a complex-engineered vehicle that needed constant attention to ensure that it functioned properly. When not at the helm, a Firefly or Tiger tank driver invariably was busy tinkering with the engine, fine-tuning its delicate mechanisms, mainly as a preventative effort. Similarly, the wireless operator would spend long hours cleaning and overhauling the mechanisms of the radio set. The other crew members would spend long hours inspecting the vehicle – checking for signs of leaks, scrutinizing the tracks for signs of damage and assessing whether the road wheels were adequately lubricated. Each day at least three crew members would repeatedly have to ram the long cleaning rod down the gun barrel to remove any tiny impurities that had accumulated in the rifling.

The entire crew also mucked in with the tasks of checking that all their items had been stowed safely internally and externally. Everyone also helped out with the time-consuming fine art of camouflaging the tank. As Unteroffizier (Corporal) Westphal's crew in the Panzer Lehr Division discovered, this even involved replacing every twig that had slipped from its original position, or straightening every blade of corn squashed down by the tank's tracks, to stop it being observed by aerial reconnaissance. Though these tasks were tedious in the extreme, most crews – despite their ribald complaints – fully understood their importance; after all, a failure of just one of these systems could easily result in the death of them all. Thus many tank crews lavished the

The crews of 1NY Sherman No. 51 'Helmdon' and No. 52, as well as Firefly No. 54 'Hanging Houghton' (all from 'C' Squadron's No. 3 Troop), preparing for the start of Operation *Totalize* on 7 August 1944. Sergeant Wilkins distributes rations while behind him sits Sherman No. 51 'Helmdon'. (IWM B8796)

same degree of love and attention on their mechanical beast as did the cavalryman of old on his charger and the infantryman on his rifle.

In terms of combat tactics, Firefly and Tiger commanders were both trained to engage enemy anti-tank guns or tanks at 800–1,200m range. The powerful cannon mounted on both tanks, however, could obtain a hit at distances up to and beyond 2,000m and – with some good fortune – disable or even knock out the enemy tank at such long ranges. Their training and combat experiences led Firefly and Tiger commanders to strive to attack the enemy's more vulnerable side or rear armour, whilst protecting their own less well-protected side and rear plates from enemy fire. This could be most readily achieved, if the battlefield situation was conducive, by assuming a concealed ambush position and knocking out the unsuspecting enemy from the flank or rear. One British Firefly ace, Sgt Wilfred Harris of the 4th/7th Dragoon Guards, managed to accomplish this with spectacular results near Villers Bocage on 14 June.

A tank commander's ability to freely observe the battlefield was a crucial factor in determining a successful outcome to an encounter with an enemy tank. However, with the commander safely battened down in the turret with his cupola hatch closed, he could only see various parts of the battlefield – a series of compass points – through his armoured visors or periscopes. Experienced Tiger and Firefly commanders like Wittmann and Gordon soon learned the value of going into action with their heads sticking up through the open turret cupola providing a good field of vision for observation of the battlefield.

Two of the crew of a Fort Garry Horse Sherman – Corporal R. Young (left) and Sgt G.E. Murray (right) – repair damage to one of the tank's tracks. (PA-137140)

FIREFLY ACE WILFRED HARRIS

Although the British Army produced fewer tank aces during World War II than the Wehrmacht, this was not due to a lack of British service personnel who possessed the same degree of tactical acumen as the Tiger commanders such as Michael Wittmann. Rather, this dearth arose because for most of the war British tanks did not mount main armaments that outclassed the enemy. Even when a comparable gun was present – as with the Firefly – these tanks only served during the last 11 months of the war and then only in small numbers. Most German aces, moreover, served in Tiger tanks, whose massive armour provided their crews with a level of survivability not available to British crews.

Therefore it is all the more creditable that – despite these obstacles – a few British Firefly commanders demonstrated their combat prowess on the battlefields of North-West Europe. Once such ace was Sgt Wilfred Harris. Born in 1911 in Walsall, Harris joined the 4th/7th Dragoon Guards during the inter-war years. A stickler for maintaining standards, Harris's immaculate appearance earned him the sobriquet 'Spit' – from that familiar army phrase 'spit and polish'. After leaving the regiment in 1935, he re-enlisted on the outbreak of war. After serving with the Motor Troop of 'A' Squadron during the disastrous 1940 campaign in France, Harris came through the evacuation from Dunkirk unscathed. Subsequently, he retrained as a tank commander, and by early 1944 was a much-respected veteran troop sergeant. In June 1944, the 4th/7th Dragoon Guards were committed to battle in Normandy as part of the independent 8th Armoured brigade. On the morning of 14 June, the regiment supported a successful attack launched by the 9th Durham Light Infantry (part of 50th Division) to secure the village of Lingèvres, near Tilly-sur-Seulles.

Subsequently, the three Shermans of No. 4 troop, 'A' Squadron – plus Sgt Harris's attached Firefly – joined the infantry in assuming defensive positions within the village. Observing with binoculars from his Firefly's open cupola, Harris spotted two Panthers approaching Lingèvres from the east at a range of 800m. Harris's first round

destroyed the lead Panther, while his second round disabled the other. Having moved to a new firing position on the other side of the village, Harris observed three Panthers approaching from the west. From this well-concealed flanking position, Harris's Firefly dispatched all three Panthers with just three rounds. In a spectacular display of shooting, Harris and his gunner, Trooper Mackillop, had destroyed no fewer than five Panthers with the same number of rounds. For this action, Harris received a richly deserved promotion to squadron quartermaster-sergeant and an award of the Distinguished Conduct Medal. After the war Harris served with the War Office police, before passing away in 1988.

It was generally only through such a quick panoramic visual scan of the battlefield with the naked eye or with binoculars that a Tiger or Firefly commander could fulfil his doctrinal training: to be the first to get a round off in an engagement, or – more critically – to be the first to hit the enemy. To achieve this, both German and Allied tank training focused on two main things: getting the commander to appraise the situation and make a swift, correct decision, and, once an order to fire had been issued, to instil a smooth and rapid working relationship between commander, gunner and loader. Thus, good tank commanders usually went into battle with their heads exposed to enemy fire; some of them paid for their professional commitment through sustaining injuries – even death – that may have been avoided if they had sought the sanctuary of a battened-down turret. During the 8 August battle with Wittmann, for example, Sgt Gordon may have been concussed when a Tiger round apparently hit a glancing blow to his open cupola hatch, bringing the armoured piece crashing agonizingly down onto his head.

While a tank commander at least had some opportunity to scan the battlefield if his cupola hatch was open, the rest of the crew enjoyed only very limited observation. The driver had the best field of vision through his relatively large driver's visor, while all the gunner saw of the outside world was through his small monocular or binocular gunnery sight. Throughout the war, the Zeiss optics fitted to German tanks, including the Tiger, were consistently excellent, and this contributed to the accuracy of the Tiger's 88mm gun, even at long ranges. The loader, of course, could see nothing of the outside world. Thus, while not the most technically challenging role in a tank, the loader needed to possess a certain personality. A loader required extreme stoicism to withstand the psychological pressures that derived from spending most of his time incarcerated in a metal box with no view of the outside world or of the enemy that threatened his life. While his survival undoubtedly depended on the rapidity and fluency with which he placed shells into the gun chamber, there was little else he could do to alter his fate, which rested in the hands of his crew mates.

A Tiger or Firefly crew, therefore, spent much of their time carrying out the often mind-numbingly tedious routine calls of duty that occurred between the few fleeting moments of intense action. These ranged from mounting guard, carrying out maintenance, observing the battlefield, refuelling and taking on ammunition, to camouflaging the vehicle and undergoing refresher training. Beyond these routine duties, the tanker's world was dominated by thoughts of food, drink, sleep and – of course – women. Usually crouched behind their tank for protection from unexpected enemy fire, Tiger and Firefly crews utilized the issued gas-stove to warm up their rations. Most Firefly crews received 'Compo Packs' – designed to provide sustenance for 14 men for one day. Each pack contained pre-prepared meal pouches, tinned vegetables and fruit, cigarettes, powdered soup and 84 sheets of toilet paper. A lucky few occasionally received that famous invention, the self-heating soup tin! To supplement these often tasteless offerings, Firefly crews often went 'foraging' to 'appropriate' or barter for local supplies: eggs, poultry, cheese and alcohol. Cigarettes and chocolate were the main currency of the barter system, but almost anything could be – and was – used in this unofficial world of commercial exchange.

Many a crewman awoke in the morning with a sore head after sampling the potent local Normandy farm cider or Calvados, with its characteristic kick. A warm cup of tea, of course, was crucial to the continued effectiveness of Firefly crews. Most found the issued 'Compo' tea – pre-mixed with powdered milk and sugar – extremely unpalatable. Much experimentation took place with additives and/or heating procedures to get the least awful brew from this unpleasant concoction. Luckily, in Normandy Firefly crews encountered hundreds of cows abandoned by their owners that provided much-welcomed fresh milk.

Whether the day had involved vicious and deadly action, or routine chores, by evening the thoughts of a Tiger or Firefly crew increasingly turned to the big question – getting some decent sleep. British armoured regiments generally followed doctrine by withdrawing behind the front to leaguer for the night in an all-round defensive position. Designated crews took it in turns to remain on full alert, fully dressed in their tanks, whilst their comrades settled down to sleep on a complementary rota basis. Some German units leaguered in much the same way, while others remained in the front – particularly when on the defensive – to support the infantrymen. Whatever the exact arrangement, sleep for a tanker could only be obtained after digging the essential foxhole or trench. Some crews dug their shelters under the tank to get extra protection, while others – fearful of the tank sinking slowly into the ground to crush them – dug theirs adjacent to their vehicle. Few got much sleep, disturbed as they were by the bustle of crews going on or returning from sentry duty, by harassing enemy artillery fire, enemy aircraft flying overhead, or just the plethora of flies and insects that assailed them during those short and warm Normandy summer nights. Long hours of tedious maintenance and camouflaging, of sleepless anxiety-filled nights, were periodically punctuated by a few brief and emotion-laden minutes of action-packed encounters with enemy armour.

THE ACTION

From their vantage point in a barn just to the north of Gaumesnil, Meyer and Waldmüller could observe the Allied lines to the north. This shot looks north-east from the barn across the main Caen–Falaise road towards Cramesnil (on the left horizon) and St-Aignan (right). The church in the latter village is just visible above the trees in the right background. (Author's collection)

As *Hitlerjugend* commander Kurt Meyer and his subordinate Hans Waldmüller observed the battlefield from their vantage point near Gaumesnil, shortly before noon on 8 August 1944, they would have seen how Simonds's *Totalize* offensive had smashed in the German front during the previous night and his reserve armour was prepared to move forward that morning. Simonds's forces were ready to strike south as soon as the approaching strategic bombers had crushed the reserve German defence line. The situation was critical – if the Allied armour struck south it would rupture the as-yet still thinly manned German reserve position and charge south to capture Falaise. Simonds's forces might subsequently thrust south to link up with the north-westerly advance of American forces from Argentan, enveloping an entire German Army in what would become known as the Falaise Pocket. Meyer knew he had but

one choice – to throw whatever meagre forces he had in the vicinity into a desperate, probably suicidal, charge north into the Allied lines. Despite facing enormous odds, Meyer hoped that through the sacrifice of his forces, he might buy some precious time to enable other German units to move north and shore up the largely unmanned second defensive line. And so at around noon, Meyer ordered his forces to initiate an improvised counter-strike against the Allied line at St-Aignan-de-Cramesnil, a riposte he demanded commence in just 30 minutes' time.

Unfortunately for Meyer, he had few forces available in the vicinity to initiate this audacious impromptu response. Operating under Waldmüller's command, this scratch force was a composite of several units. The infantry component comprised 500 Panzergrenadiers from I Battalion, SS Regiment 25. The stiffening element for this force came from 20 tanks (mostly Panzer IVs) from SS Panzer Regiment 12. The vanguard of the counter-strike, however, was formed from four or five (one source suggests seven) Tigers from SS-Hauptsturmführer Michael Wittmann's 2nd Company, 101st SS Heavy Tank Battalion. Meyer placed most of his hopes that this desperate mission might achieve success through the lethal firepower and proven battlefield survivability of these few Tigers. Although the evidence concerning the composition of this Tiger force is contradictory, it is certain that most of the tanks were from Wittmann's own troop. However, a mass of Allied units faced this weak German strike force. In the La Jalousie–St-Aignan sector the Allies deployed three armoured regiments and four infantry battalions, not to mention the spearhead of two armoured divisions

1NY tank crews complete preparations for the forthcoming *Totalize* offensive near Cormelles on 7 August. In the foreground is a Sherman (Hybrid) while behind this the long barrel of the second tank identifies it as a Firefly. (IWM B8805)

assembling behind them. Although only a small proportion of these tanks could bring their fire to bear on Wittmann's Tigers, his armoured column was clearly about to charge north into an inferno of Allied tank, anti-tank and artillery defensive fire.

At the moment when Meyer ordered Waldmüller to initiate this ad-hoc counter-attack, Wittmann was in his Tiger, alongside three others, located in the Les Jardinets area, 600m east-south-east of Meyer's Gaumesnil vantage point. One of the major benefits to the Germans in their defensive role was their familiarity with the territory. Carefully camouflaged, the drivers had hidden their Tigers behind by a typical tall Normandy tree-hedge line; the row of low bushes running along the other side of this narrow dirt lane added to this concealment. At around 1205 hours, Wittmann heard that Meyer had urgently summoned him to a briefing at nearby Cintheaux. Wittmann's driver steered Tiger 007 west down country lanes for a few minutes to arrive at the village. Jumping down from his turret, Wittmann found Meyer and Waldmüller settling the final details of the counter-strike, outlining the part Wittman's Tigers would play in the action.

According to Meyer, a dramatic event then occurred that transformed the timeframe for the intended attack. The three SS officers observed a solitary Allied heavy bomber fly over Cintheaux, sending out coloured flares. This was obviously an Allied Pathfinder designating the aim points for an impending strategic bombing strike. Given what

A Firefly seen within a long column of armour from the 1st Polish Armoured Division begins to move south to spearhead the second phase of *Totalize* on the morning of 8 August 1944. (IWM B8826)

Meyer already knew about Allied Pathfinder tactics from the earlier Normandy battles, he knew that the heavy bombers were already less than ten minutes away from their current location. It was obvious to all that the Allied armour assembling behind the current front line had not commenced its assault south because they were waiting for heavy bombers to unleash a rain of destruction on the German forces below.

This realization merely confirmed Meyer's recent decision to strike north. If his forces remained where they currently were, they would be obliterated by hundreds of tons of high explosive. No doubt, as his dazed forces struggled to recover from this onslaught, the massed Allied armoured formations would surge south to overwhelm them. The second German line would swiftly collapse and there would be nothing to stop an Allied advance to Falaise and beyond; the collapse of the already reeling German front in Normandy might ensue. Meyer again ordered them to launch the attack – but now to do so immediately. Despite the appalling odds facing his mission, Wittmann climbed into his tank and headed east back to his company's positions in Les Jardinets. Within minutes, his force of four Tigers had shaken off their camouflage and had begun to advance north across the open fields towards the Allied lines. A few hundred metres further east, a fifth Tiger (and possibly two others) also began to rumble north. Over the ensuing hour Wittmann and his Tigers bravely attempted to wrest an improbable victory from the jaws of defeat.

OVERLEAF
Firefly commanded by Lt James engages the Tiger of Michael Wittman at a range of 800m. The Tiger exploded so powerfully that the entire turret was thrown clear of the wrecked chassis.

Shermans of the 1st Polish Armoured Division form up ready to advance south on 8 August. (IWM B8823)

ADVANCE TO ST-AIGNAN

One of the Allied units deployed in the La Jalousie–St-Aignan sector would play a key role in defeating Wittmann's riposte. The 1NY was a Sherman-equipped armoured regiment in the independent British 33rd Armoured Brigade. Led by Lt-Col D. Forster, the regiment fielded three squadrons – 'A', 'B' and 'C', plus the regimental headquarters. Most of the regiment's tanks bore distinctive names; 'A' Squadron's were named after Soviet towns, 'B' Squadron's after American states, and 'C' Squadron's after Northamptonshire villages. The regiment's authorized strength was 59 Shermans, including 12 Fireflies.

As part of the 'Left British column', which also comprised the infantry of the 1st Black Watch (1BW), the 1NY had advanced 6km to St-Aignan during the early hours of 8 August. Having assembled in a 50-vehicle-deep by four-vehicle-wide formation, the column's advance commenced around midnight. At 0130 hours, No. 2 Troop, 'A' Squadron, which had detached from the rest of the column, stumbled upon four well-camouflaged enemy self-propelled guns (SPGs) and a fierce action ensued that demonstrated the Firefly's killing power. Four rounds hit Lt Jones's lead Sherman No. 5 'Brest-Litovsk'; one tore off the external blanket bin, another penetrated to lodge in the vehicle's transmission gear, the third gouged a groove out of the frontal armour before bouncing away, and the fourth smashed through to the engine. With the tank on fire, Sgt Burnett's IC (Hybrid) Firefly No. 8 'Balaclava' engaged the three SPGs. The Firefly dispatched two of them with three rounds, but not before the third SPG had knocked out the troop's two remaining standard Shermans. While the sole

Lt Brown, the commander of No. 4 Troop, 'C' Squadron, 1NY, uses a map to brief crews about the forthcoming night infiltration to St-Aignan. Looming behind them is Brown's own tank, standard Sherman No. 55 'Lillingstone', which was lost the next day during the battle for Le Petit Ravin. (IWM B8798)

survivor – Burnett's Firefly – caught up with the column, the three dismounted crews endured the rest of the night pinned to the ground by machine gun fire. Lt Jones had previously written to his mother telling her not to worry, but during this ordeal he said out loud '… for goodness sake Mother start worrying now!'

Subsequently, the column rumbled on until, at 0325 hours, it reached a hedge situated north of its objective, St-Aignan. Accompanied by artillery fire, two Sherman squadrons pushed through gaps in the hedge and engaged the enemy, while the now-dismounted infantry stormed the village. After an hour-long battle, the column captured St-Aignan and began establishing firm defensive positions around it. As part of this process, 'A' Squadron assumed defensive positions in the orchards located south-west of St-Aignan at Delle de la Roque. At this stage the regiment fielded 54 operational Shermans, including the 12 Fireflies, having lost four standard Shermans during the night advance; a fifth tank – Sgt Duff's No. 56 'Lamport' – ended up with the 144th RAC at Cramesnil.

WITTMANN'S DEATH CHARGE

At around 1220 hours, therefore, Wittmann's troop of four Tigers began to advance north from Les Jardinets. That day, Wittmann was not in his usual vehicle, Tiger 205, which was being repaired. Instead, he was using battalion commander Heinz von Westernhagen's Command Tiger, number 007. Apart from Tiger 007, it is

The 12th SS-Panzer Division *Hitlerjugend* was a direct product of Hitler Youth indoctrination and training. Thrown into the action against British and Canadian troops in June 1944, it performed very well. These young Panzergrenadiers of the division are shown receiving medals less than two weeks after the D-Day landings. (Ullstein)

probable that the column comprised Ihrion's Tiger 314, Dollinger's 008, and Blase's tank – the exact composition of and the order within this formation remains unclear. The tanks rumbled north-north-west, one behind the other, on an axis parallel to, but around 150m east of, the main Caen–Falaise road. That Wittmann's column was in line ahead suggests that he expected enemy fire from the north around Hill 122. This deployment, however, left the Tigers' more vulnerable flanks exposed to fire from the north-east – from the orchards of Delle de la Roque, south-west of St-Aignan. Wittmann remained unaware that 'A' Squadron, 1NY, was positioned in these woods.

Both Meyer and his medical officer, SS-Hauptsturmführer Dr Wolfgang Rabe, observed the initial stages of Wittmann's advance. The Tigers rumbled north through a hail of Allied defensive artillery fire. The tanks only stopped periodically in shallow gullies to fire at long range towards the north-west to engage Sherbrooke Fusilier tanks located west of the main road. At a range of 1800m, the Tigers knocked out several Shermans, whereas at this distance only the Canadian regiment's few Fireflies stood a slim chance of destroying the Tigers. Having observed the first phase of Wittmann's charge from the northern fringes of Cintheaux, Meyer's attention was now diverted to the northern horizon. Suddenly, the sky to the north began to darken as what seemed to be an endless stream of Allied bombers droned south towards the village. Meyer and the grenadiers dug in around him were rendered speechless by this display of vast Allied

8 AUGUST 1944, 1247 HOURS

+ 20 SECONDS

On receipt of orders from the tank commander, Lieutenant James, the Firefly's gunner – Trooper Ekins – begins to lay the 17-pounder gun on the target, Wittman's Tiger.

With the Tiger in the cross-hairs, Ekins calculates the range – around 800m and the loader places an AP round in the breech. As James counts down "3 – 2 – 1 – fire!", the crew places their hands over their ears, open their mouths and close their eyes – all in preparation for the violent back blast.

air power. 'What an honour,' remarked one, 'Churchill is sending a bomber for each of us!' The SS grenadiers raced across the open fields located north of the village to escape the impending onslaught. Just in time, they witnessed the bombers pass over them and begin dropping their bombs onto the village behind them.

Deployed behind the cover provided by the tall tree-lined hedge that marked the southern border of the Delle de la Roque orchards, the four tanks of 'A' Squadron's No. 3 Troop held the westernmost part of the 1NY defensive position. Led by Lieutenant James in Tank No. 9, a Standard Sherman, the troop also deployed two more standard Shermans – Sgt Eley 's No. 10 'Vladivostock' and Cpl Hillaby's No. 11. The troop's last and most potent asset was Sgt Gordon's VC Firefly No. 12, according to some sources, named 'Velikye Luki'. Straining to see through the gaps in the tree-hedge, the Troop's observers peered south across the open ground towards the Les Jardinets area. Three Tigers were heading north-north-east in line ahead, on an axis just east of the main road. The range was 1200m. Gordon reported this sighting via radio to Captain Boardman, the Squadron second-in-command. Boardman claims that he then ordered Gordon to hold his fire until he could get there to direct the action. Why the captain did not instruct the Squadron's three other Fireflies to reinforce Gordon's tank remains a mystery. Moving west through the orchard in his Sherman I, No. 18 'Omsk', Boardman soon arrived at the No. 3 Troop position. By this time rather random German artillery and mortar fire was landing in the general area of the orchard.

+ 30 SECONDS

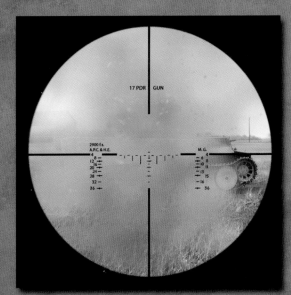

The gun is fired and within a second the round has smashed into the Tiger. For a few seconds, however, this fact remains unknown to the Firefly crew, as they are momentarily blinded by the flash and back blast.

+ 50 SECONDS

Just a few seconds later, and the crews have adjusted to the now subsided blast. Looking through his gunsight, Ekins can see smoke rising from the Tiger. A few more seconds pass and then Ekins sees the Tiger erupt as its ammunition explodes.

The British observed the advancing Tigers for a couple of minutes. The enemy seemed to be unaware of the British tanks' presence, as the Tigers still remained deployed in line ahead on a bearing north-north-east, which exposed their relatively less formidable side armour to No. 3 Troop's tanks. Convinced that they were undetected, the Troop calmly allowed the Tigers to advance until the range had closed to 800m, by which time the tanks had neared the vicinity of the isolated red-roofed building adjacent to the main road. At this range, Gordon's Firefly stood a good chance of penetrating the Tiger's side armour, although the other Shermans still stood virtually no chance at all. The time was now 1239 hours. According to Gordon's gunner, Trooper Joe Ekins, the sergeant now told the other Shermans to stay under cover while he courageously attempted to deal with the Tigers.

Gordon ordered his driver to move the Firefly forward a few metres to a position just in front of (that is, south of) the orchard's southern edge to obtain a better field of fire. Gordon remained with his head poking through the open commander's cupola during the ensuing brief action. Gordon selected his target – the rear Tiger of the three, as was normal practice; such a tactic hoped to exploit the fact that the leading tanks might not even know that their rear colleague had been hit. The reason why British accounts only mention three Tigers, when Wittmann's column may well have had four or five, remains unclear. Some of the Tigers may have dropped out of the column and were heading north-north-east on an axis to the left (west) of the others and may even have been obscured from view. The time was now 1240 hours. Looking through his sight, gunner Ekins was now very frightened because he believed that there 'was no way' a solitary Firefly could take on three Tigers and survive. With 'but one thought in my mind – to get the bastard before he gets you' – Ekins aimed the gun and fired two armour-piercing rounds at the rear Tiger. Despite having only fired

six 17-pounder rounds before, Ekins nevertheless had 'a knack' at gunnery, and both rounds seemingly hit the target; within seconds, the Tiger was burning. Other Allied tanks, however, were also engaging the Tigers at this time. The Canadian Fireflies of the Sherbrooke Foresters were firing from their positions west of the main road at a range of 1100m. Similarly, 144th RAC Fireflies, located on Hill 122, were engaging Tigers at a range of 1300m. While it is not impossible that this longer-range fire hit and penetrated the Tiger at precisely the same as Ekins engaged it, the most likely explanation is that Ekins's rounds penetrated the tank and caused it to burn.

As soon as the Firefly had fired its second shot, Gordon followed doctrine by ordering the driver to reverse back into the cover of the orchard. As they did so, the second Tiger traversed its gun right towards the Firefly. Looking through his sight, Ekins recalled that the Tiger's 88mm gun 'looked as big as a battleship' as it swung to face him. The Tiger fired a round at the Firefly as it began to reverse and then a further two rounds as the tank entered the concealment of the apple orchard. As the third round passed close by the tank, the flap of the open commander's cupola came crashing down onto Gordon's head, knocking him half-senseless. It is not clear if this was caused by the flap knocking into a tree-branch or because the Tiger's round had actually hit it a glancing blow. The dazed Gordon clambered uneasily down from his tank and was immediately wounded by shrapnel, as the German artillery and mortar fire moved closer to the tree-hedge. All Ekins knew of this incident was that suddenly there was no commander in his tank!

Next, the commander of No. 3 Troop – Lt James – bravely jumped out of his tank and raced across to take command of the Firefly. James ordered the driver to move the tank to a new firing position. The tank reached this new position just before 1247 hours, according to the war diary entry. Moving out from cover, James now ordered

One of the 1NY's Fireflies in action. This photograph shows the Sherman IC Firefly No. 32 'New Orleans' of No. 2 Troop, 'B' Squadron. The image was taken on 17 July 1944 in the Odon valley sector of the front. (IWM B7423)

Ekins to engage the second Tiger – the one that had fired at the Firefly. At 1247 hours Ekins fired one shot at the second tank, which hit it, causing it to explode in a ball of flame. As the tank Wittmann was believed to be in – command Tiger 007 – was found with its turret blown off, and German eyewitness reports recorded only one exploding tank, it seems likely that this was the precise moment at which Wittmann's prolific career was terminated. Next, Gordon's driver again reversed the Firefly back into the cover of the orchard. This success just left intact the lead Tiger and the mystery fourth and fifth Tigers, which the British accounts of the battle seem to have missed altogether.

At this juncture, it is claimed that some standard Shermans advanced south out of the woods to engage the remaining Tigers at such close range that they stood some chance of damaging them, but this inadvertently hampered the fire delivered by Ekins's Firefly, which had re-emerged out of the orchard. The ensuing hail of 75mm Sherman fire apparently fell upon the lead enemy tank. While these rounds failed to penetrate the tank's thick armour, the hail of fire caused the driver to veer off erratically to the west, seemingly out of control. According to the regimental historian this tank 'was in a panic, milling around wondering how he could escape'. Captain Boardman then claims that he engaged the veering Tiger with a 75mm armour-piercing round that caused it to stop. Ekins, however, states that 'it was still moving when I hit him'. Ekins fired two shots that caused the Tiger to burst into flames; from this inferno none of the crew escaped. The time was 1252 hours. The final successes of this action also went to the Firefly. Just eight minutes later, at 1300 hours, Sgt Finney's Firefly – Tank No. 4 'Orenburg' – spotted two Panzer IVs moving to the west side of the main road at the prodigious range of 1645m. In a brilliant piece of shooting, gunner Trooper Crittenden fired two shots and brewed up both Panzers.

Wittmann's death charge had been a remarkable action. As Ekins well knew, the chances of a solitary Firefly surviving a clash not with just one but with at least three

View taken from the location where Wittman's Tiger was destroyed, close to the red-roofed building by the main road, looking north-east towards the tree-hedge at Delle de la Roque (which in 1944 was less substantial). Ekins's Firefly was located just west of this hedge, on the fringes of the apple orchard that extended to the western entrance of Le Petit Ravin. Behind the hedge, the spire of St-Aignan church is just visible above the trees. (Author's collection SH-7/3)

(and possibly five) Tigers were extraordinarily slim. Yet in the space of just 12 minutes, Gordon's Firefly had dispatched three Tigers with just five rounds. In return, not only did the Tigers not even knock out a single enemy tank, but it seems as if not one of the rounds they fired hit its target. This astounding feat was one of the finest tank-versus-tank engagements seen during the entire North-West Europe campaign. It seems odd, therefore, that none of his peers congratulated Ekins for this feat, even though the gunner maintains that he never expected it anyway. The accomplishment also deserves more recognition than the laconic note penned in the regiment's war diary: 'Three Tigers in twelve minutes is not bad business.' The combination of three factors – the regiment's use of terrain to ambush the Tigers, Gordon's 'knack' at gunnery and the Firefly's awesome gun had turned the dispatching of one of Germany's finest aces from an almost impossible task into something 'rather like Practice No. 5 on the ranges at Linney Head'.

What then was Wittmann's fate? Dr Rabe had observed this short but bloody battle from the western side of the main road. He recalled that the four or five Tigers involved had come under enemy fire and that several had gone up in flames. He attempted to get closer to see if any of the crews had survived, but could not because of enemy fire. After waiting for two hours, not a single crew member had emerged from the battlefield, and so Rabe withdrew, assuming that all had been killed. Wittmann was officially listed as missing in action.

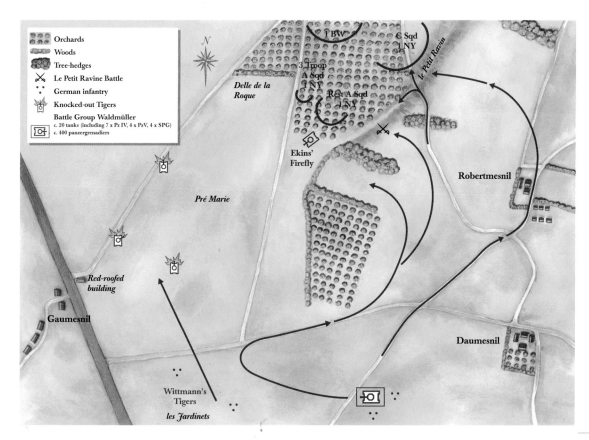

THE BATTLE FOR LE PETIT RAVIN

Shortly afterwards, a few hundred metres further east, another fierce tank-versus-tank action occurred. Although there were no Tigers involved, this action again attested to the increasingly value that the British could place on the potent Firefly. Around 1255 hours, 'A' Squadron spotted 20 German tanks – mostly Panzer IVs but with some Panthers too – heading west across Les Jardinets towards the main road at a range of 1,200m. The tanks moved along the various tree-hedges in the area, which largely obscured them. Ekins fired one round at the leading tank. In another piece of superb marksmanship, the round hit, causing the tank to burst into flames. With other Shermans joining in, the Panzers scuttled into cover. Some then used the tree-hedges around Daumesnil to move north unobserved until they reached the eastern end of Le Petit Ravin, a steep-sided defile located south of St-Aignan. Some Panzers then infiltrated west along this narrow gully, while others advanced to the south of it, to attack elements of 'A' and 'C' Squadrons.

A fierce and confused battle now raged in and around the gully. Early on, Ekins's Firefly took a hit from a Panzer. Knowing the Sherman's tendency to burn, the crew swiftly baled out. A terrified Ekins, with fire erupting all around him, ran northwards towards the sanctuary of St-Aignan. Subsequently, a Panzer IV took up a well-concealed position in the ravine, with only its turret visible to the British, and quickly dispatched three Shermans. Major Skelton, the 'A' Squadron commander, instructed Sgt Moralee's Firefly No. 16 'Kursk' to take out the troublesome tank by flanking round to the left. As Moralee attempted to locate the well-hidden Panzer, the latter fired twice and hit 'Kursk', causing it to burn. Skelton angrily snarled, 'we are not going to let this bastard pick off the Squadron one by one', and ordered Sgt Finney's Firefly No. 4 'Orenburg' to join him in a pincer movement. The Firefly bravely drew the Panzer's fire, being brewed up in the process, which allowed Skelton's No. 17 'Tomsk' to approach the German tank unnoticed from the other side and knock it out

A view taken from in front of the tree-hedge at Delle de le Roque, looking south-west towards the red-roofed building adjacent to the main Caen–Falaise road. Wittman's tank was knocked out near this building. (Author's collection SH-6/36)

with a single close-range shot. The normally imperturbable Skelton, however, was so enraged by the casualties inflicted on his crews by the Panzer that he then ordered his gunner to pour a further six rounds into the stricken vehicle. This onslaught of hot metal obliterated both the tank and its entire crew.

A little later, the Panzer IV driven by SS-Sturmmann (Junior Corporal) Helmut Wiese, from the 5th Company, II Battalion, SS Panzer Regiment 12, was in the thick of the action near the gully. As they approached the British positions, Wiese described how the crew's nerves were stretched to breaking point as they experienced the violent rattle of British machine gun and rifle fire striking the tank. Spotting 1BW infantry moving an anti-tank gun into position in a nearby copse, the tank commander ordered the driver to reverse the tank at full speed, while the gunner unleashed several HE rounds towards the wood. Suddenly, an anti-tank round smashed into the tank, with a 'bang as if a soda pop bottle had smashed into a stone floor'. As flames consumed the stricken vehicle, Wiese baled out, his uniform on fire, but the loader and the gunner both perished in the ensuing inferno.

Next, Sgt Smith's Firefly No. 40 'New Jersey' engaged a Panzer IV located 1500m away on the Robertmesnil Ridge. It took Trooper Coleman four shots to find the mark, however, but the end result was a burning Panzer. Smith then spotted and engaged another Panzer IV. Coleman's first round smashed through the tank's armour, causing it to burn and then explode as its ammunition went up; the tank promptly collapsed into 'a junk heap of twisted, red hot, metal'. By this time, the remaining German tanks and infantry were retreating in disarray. The combination of the fire from Firefly and ordinary Shermans, anti-tank guns, and supporting artillery had driven back the German counter-attack. According to Allied accounts, 16 knocked-out German AFVs littered the battlefield around Le Petit Ravin, of which the Firefly had bagged seven. The up-gunned Sherman had proved its ability to vanquish not just the ordinary Panzer IV, but also the most-feared German heavy tank, the Tiger. From this duel at St-Aignan – probably the last great clash of Firefly versus Tiger – the Firefly emerged triumphant.

The western exit of the Le Petit Ravin ('the gully'), as seen from the 1NY positions south of St-Aignan. This view is deceptive, as it disguises the width and depth of the gully. Ekins's Firefly was off to the left of this shot. (Author's collection SH-6/34)

That evening, a surreal epitaph to the day's events transpired. As darkness emerged, the surviving 1NY tanks gathered to leaguer for the night north of St-Aignan. Replacement 75mm Shermans and personnel moved forward to rebuild the badly damaged unit. Within 'A' Squadron, Captain Boardman needed to find a wireless operator for one of the replacement 75mm-gunned Sherman. Luckily, a number of the surviving personnel were well trained in several disciplines. One gunner in particular was qualified as a wireless operator. And so that night, Boardman 'rewarded' Ekins for his spectacular gunnery achievements that day. The captain allocated Ekins to one of the new replacement 75mm-gunned Shermans – as its wireless operator.

THE CONTROVERSIES OF WAR

A view taken from within the gully. The combination of the ravine's steep sides and the number of apple trees made this difficult terrain for tanks to operate in; nevertheless a bitter tank action raged here during the early afternoon of 8 August. (Author's collection SH-10/4a)

Many events that occur in battle are subject to different interpretations thanks to the inherent fog of war and the differing deductions made from the available evidence. Nowhere is this more evident than when famous wartime figures meet their death in battle. Given Wittmann's legendary status it should not surprise us that over the last three decades controversy has raged over which unit and which weapon actually destroyed his tank. For many years after 1945, however, no one on the Allied side even realized that Wittmann had been killed during the 8 August battle, which thus remained just one of hundreds of otherwise unremarkable, half-remembered, war-time actions.

Once it became known on the Allied side that Wittmann had been a victim of this battle, the leading interpretation was that his demise had been caused by a high-explosive rocket fired from a RAF Hawker Typhoon aircraft. This interpretation was based largely on the circumstantial evidence that an unexploded rocket was found nearby, and on the specious logic that such a devastating explosion could only have been caused by such a weapon. As the doubts about this explanation mounted, a number of British and Canadian armoured regiments deployed near Gaumesnil that afternoon claimed the distinction of dispatching Wittmann; of these, the claim of the 1NY stood out as being the one best supported by convincing contemporary evidence.

The long-held suspicions about the validity of the Typhoon explanation were vindicated in 2005 by Brian Reid's excellent book *No Holding Back*. Through careful examination of 2nd Tactical Air Force logs, Reid concluded that Wittmann "almost assuredly did not fall victim to an attack from the air." While accepting the strength of the 1NY claim, the Canadian historian went on to argue that Wittmann's tank may have been knocked out by a round fired from the west by a Firefly from a Canadian unit, the Sherbrooke Fusiliers. The justification for this interpretation relies on the accuracy of a brief description of Wittmann's tank made in late 1945 by a French civilian, which might be construed as indicating a hit fired from the west. Unfortunately, the Fusiliers' war diary was destroyed on 8 August, so that there is little contemporary evidence to support this interpretation, which accepts Major Radley-Walter's subsequent insistence that he had moved his Sherbrooke Fusilier squadron forward to Gaumesnil where they engaged some Tigers.

What this conjecture leaves us with is the few uncontested known facts from the time of the battle. As we have seen, the 1NY war diary recorded three Tigers being destroyed at the exact time when and in the general location where Wittmann's Tiger was destroyed. Furthermore, the unit's account of the battle was produced within a few weeks of the battle when no one in the regiment realized the significance of what they were describing. No other competing interpretation of how Wittmann came to be killed can remotely compete with the wealth of unequivocal impartial contemporary evidence that supports the claim of the 1NY. In all probability, it was a woefully inexperienced Firefly gunner, Joe Ekins, who dispatched the veteran SS panzer ace that afternoon. Even Reid accepts that Wittmann "may well have perished" at the hands of the 1NY, while in June 2006, David Willey, curator at the Tank Museum at Bovington, UK, commented, "it is pretty much accepted now that Joe Ekins was the man who knocked out" Michael Wittmann[2].

After years of speculation as to the whereabouts of Wittmann's remains, in 1982 these were located and re-interred in the La Cambe military graveyard in Normandy. By then the Wittmann legend had become well-established and today the SS officer continues to stimulate huge public interest. In contrast, Ekins survived the war, and returned to Rushden, Northamptonshire, to live a quiet life. He worked in a shoe factory, married and had two children and for many years declined to enter discussions about what happened during the war. It now seems fitting that after all these years he has finally received some public recognition for his remarkable war service.

2   *Daily Mail* article and interview with David Willey, Joe Ekins, 2006

ANALYSIS OF THE BATTLE

For analytical purposes, the climactic battle near St-Aignan on the early afternoon of 8 August 1944 can be divided into two actions; the death charge of Wittmann's Tigers, and the confused battle that raged around Le Petit Ravin. Finally, the approach march of the British left column during the previous night can be counted as a necessary precursor to these two actions. Like all battles, a degree of confusion and contradictory evidence exists regarding these actions, but this section attempts to analyse and quantify the known facts.

One obvious feature of the battle to be analysed is the number of armoured fighting vehicles (AFVs) destroyed during these actions. Table 1 depicts the German losses suffered during these actions, according to British accounts.

Wittman's Tiger was located near the red-roofed building (present back in 1944), located adjacent to the main Caen–Falaise road, when it was hit by Gordon's Firefly. (Author's collection SH-7/2)

Sherman Fireflies suffered a heavy attrition rate in Normandy after being singled out by the enemy as the primary target of their tank fire. This photograph, taken on 6 October 1944, shows the crew of 'Alanac', the only Firefly in the Fort Garry Horse to survive from D-Day, perched on the tank's long barrel. (Ken Bell/PA-138413)

TABLE 1: GERMAN AFVS LOSSES, 7–8 AUGUST, ACCORDING TO BRITISH ACCOUNTS

Type of AFV:	Night March	Wittmann Action	Le Petit Ravin Action	Total Lost
Pz IV	0	2 [2]	7 [4]	9 [6]
Pz V Panther	0	0	4 [1]	4 [1]
Pz VI Tiger	0	5 [3]	0	5 [3]
SP Gun	2 [2]	0	4 [2]	6 [4]
Unidentified	0	0	1	1 [0]
TOTAL	**2 [2]**	**7 [5]**	**16 [7]**	**25 [14]**

(Numbers lost to Fireflies shown in square brackets)
Sources: 1NY War Diary; Abbott; Neville; Taylor (see bibliography for full details)

We also possess detailed contemporary records, or secondary accounts, about the tank losses the 1NY suffered during the battle. The regiment started *Totalize* with a full complement of 59 tanks. During the night advance to St-Aignan, as Table 2 shows, the regiment lost the services of five tanks.

TABLE 2: 1NY TANKS LOST DURING NIGHT ADVANCE

Vehicle #	Type	Trp/Sqd	Commander	Fate
2 'Odessa'	Sherman	1/A	Sgt Ryan	KO'd by Panzerfaust.
5 'Brest- Litovsk'	Sherman	2/A	Griffith-Jones	KO'd by German SPG.
6 'Bryansk'	Sherman	2/A	Sgt Jeffcoates	KO'd by German SPG.
7 'Belgorod'	Sherman	2/A	Cpl Smith	KO'd by German SPG.
56 'Lamport'				Became detached, ended up in Cramesnil

Sources: Abbott; Neville.

During the battle for Le Petit Ravin, as Table 3 shows, the 1NY lost four Fireflies and nine Standard Shermans, plus another Sherman seriously damaged but recovered. It is interesting to note that the regiment did not lose a single tank during the brief encounter with Wittmann's Tigers.

TABLE 3: 1NY TANK LOSSES DURING THE BATTLE FOR LE PETIT RAVIN

	Lost to tank fire	Lost to anti-tank fire	Vehicle number/name
Sherman	8	1*	Nos. 11, 13, 14 'Kerch', 43 'Cottesbrooke', 47 'Sulgrave', 48, 55 'Lillingstone', 61 'Brixworth'; * No. 49.
Firefly	4	0	Nos. 4 'Orenburg', 12, 16 'Kursk', 50 'Stony Stratford'
TOTALS	12	1	

Sources: 1NY War Diary; Abbott; Neville.

Another aspect worth attempting to quantify is the personnel casualties suffered during these actions. German sources provide us with only fragmentary evidence on this issue, and one can only piece together a rough estimate based on various snippets of information, as shown in Table 4. This is particularly true of the Wittmann action. It seems that all of Wittmann's crew died when Tiger 007 exploded. We do not know how many of the other four Tigers' crews escaped, although it is reasonable to assume that the entire crew of the fifth (northernmost) Tiger escaped, as it was abandoned intact. One witness to the action – Dr Rabe – did not see anyone from the crew from the three Tigers destroyed by Ekins's Firefly successfully flee the battlefield. It is reasonable from this to assume that German tank crew casualties in the Wittmann action were at least 15 killed.

TABLE 4: ESTIMATED GERMAN PERSONNEL LOSSES DURING 7–8 AUGUST BATTLES	
	Killed, wounded, missing, captured
Defence of approaches to St Aignan	60 (including 40 POWs)
Wittmann's death charge – tank crew	15+
Wittmann's death charge – Panzergrenadiers	30
Battle for Le Petit Ravin – tank crew	35+
Battle for Le Petit Ravin – Panzergrenadiers	50+
TOTAL	**190+**

Sources: 1NY War Diary; H. Meyer; K. Meyer; Neville.

British sources are more detailed in giving the number of personnel casualties the 1NY suffered during these actions, as depicted in Table 5.

One of Wittman's Tigers knocked out on 13 June 1944 at Villers Bocage, photographed on 5 August 1944 after the Allies had captured the town. The ruined state of the place was typical of many Normandy towns liberated after D-Day. (IWM B8635)

TABLE 5: 1NY PERSONNEL CASUALTIES DURING 7–8 AUGUST		
	Officers	NCOs/ ORs
Killed	2	10
Wounded	11	40
TOTAL	**13**	**50**

Notes: These figures include at least one officer, one NCO killed, and seven NCOs/ORs wounded during the night advance, but excludes 1BW casualties during the night march. *Sources: 1NY War Diary; Abbott; Neville.*

If all this data is put together, an approximate summary of the respective losses suffered during the actions of 7–8 August can be calculated, as shown in Table 6.

TABLE 6: LOSSES DURING THE 7–8 AUGUST ACTIONS AROUND ST-AIGNAN		
	Germans	1NY
AFV permanent losses	25	13
Personnel losses	190+	63

Sources: War Diaries; Abbott; H. Meyer; K. Meyer; Neville; Niemis; Taylor

THE AFTERMATH

Thanks to the Firefly, Wittmann's desperate charge north into the Allied lines near St-Aignan was repulsed and his Tigers either destroyed or abandoned. Allied Firefly and standard Sherman fire, augmented by anti-tank and artillery fire, also eventually forced back the other element of Meyer's counter-attack force in the battle that raged in and around Le Petit Ravin. Meyer's audacious attempt to block the impending Allied armoured onslaught in Phase Two of Operation *Totalize* had failed. The Allied armour commenced its attack south on schedule, after the bombing ended at 1355 hours. In these circumstances, the rest of 8 August 1944 ought to have been precisely the disastrous 'black day' for the Germans that the Canadians had hoped it would be. Thanks to the Firefly, Meyer's fear that the Allies would successfully race south to occupy Falaise that day ought to have been realized.

But the spectre of disaster did not materialize. The two armoured divisions of Lt-Gen Guy Simonds's II Canadian Corps – both as yet unblooded into the horrors of combat in Normandy – advanced cautiously that afternoon, fearful of the long-range killing power of the handful of Tigers, Panthers, Panzer IVs and 75mm anti-tank guns still available to the meagre defending German forces. The lethal firepower of such assets in such open terrain was soon demonstrated when the advancing Polish armour lost 40 tanks to German fire in the space of just 15 minutes. The defenders used the intervening time well to rush reinforcements to their severely depleted front on the Falaise plain. In fact it would take Simonds's forces another week to secure the high ground that dominated Falaise. Thus it was a combination of other factors, plus some good fortune – rather than the sacrifice of Wittmann's Tigers – that enabled the German forces to escape the debacle envisaged by Meyer that lunchtime on 8 August.

This lucky escape, however, did not alter the fate that was about to consume the Westheer in Normandy – it merely postponed it by a few days. By mid-August,

Vehicles of the 4th Canadian Armoured Division assemble ready to advance south during the afternoon of 8 August 1944. (Ken Bell/ PA-113650)

Simonds's forces had pushed forward beyond Falaise to link up with the Americans near Trun to close the Falaise pocket. Undoubtably the Allies had won a great victory. The German's Seventh Army and the greater part of the Fifth Army had been destroyed with the loss of thousands of German soldiers. Although many German troops escaped with some armour and guns towards the Seine no significant German forces remained to face the Allies after the loss of Normandy. In the ensuing weeks the Allies rampaged forward all the way to the borders of the Reich. There seemed a remote and fleeting opportunity that the war might be won during 1944. However, Allied logistical exhaustion and rapid German recovery ensured that the Allies would have to grind their way through Germany in a series of bitter battles that would rage into early 1945. By then – with nearly half the British spearhead armour being Fireflies and with very few Tigers still operational – the predictable German collapse ensued. On 8 May the Nazi German regime surrendered unconditionally to the Allies.

So what did the summer 1944 battle for Normandy – and particularly Wittmann's 8 August 1944 death charge – prove about the epic clash of Firefly versus Tiger? The Normandy campaign aptly displayed the weaknesses of the expedient Firefly design. With armour identical to the standard Sherman, the Firefly remained vulnerable to enemy tank and anti-tank fire. It took great bravery from Sherman crews to go into action against the latest generation of powerfully gunned Panzers, especially given the Sherman's legendary tendency to burn when hit. Yet equally, the campaign – and the 8 August action in particular – showed that, in the Firefly, Allied armoured units had finally got the 'Panzer killer' they required. These battles showed that the Firefly could take on and defeat all of Germany's latest tanks, including the much-feared Tiger. The

battle that raged near St-Aignan on 8 August represented the Firefly's finest hour. With careful concealment and courageous patience, the 1NY ambushed Wittmann's desperate charge north. In a matter of minutes, a single Firefly had dispatched three Tigers with just five rounds, in the process dispatching one of Germany's leading tank aces.

In August 1944, therefore, the Firefly and the Tiger were the dominant tanks on the battlefields of North-West Europe. Yet this dominance was short-lived. While from the perspective of Normandy the Firefly emerged as the victor and the Tiger the vanquished, both at this time also shared a growing sense of approaching demise. With its production ended and the tank now outclassed by the King Tiger, the Tiger would appear on the battlefield in decreasing numbers until the end of the war. So too the Firefly; with production ended in May 1945, it was soon replaced by specifically designed medium tanks like the Comet that were better armed and armoured. The Firefly was, after all, just an expedient – albeit an economical, effective and well-timed one. Without its lethal firepower, it is possible that the Westheer may have been able to maintain a coherent front in Normandy for much longer than they did. Sherman Fireflies were indeed, as reports at the time suggested, 'battle-deciding weapons … everyone of which … will help materially to shorten the war'.

A knocked-out White M3A1 Scout car and, behind it, a Crusader anti-aircraft tank lay knocked out in a field near Bretteville-le-Rabet at the start of Simonds's *Tractable* offensive on 14 August. (PA-1137505)

BIBLIOGRAPHY

PRIMARY SOURCES (UNPUBLISHED)

Author's correspondence with Mr Joe Ekins, 2006

Imperial War Museum Sound Archive
Taped interviews with Trooper Ekins and Captain Boardman

The National Archives, Kew, London
CAB 106/1047, British Army of the Rhine Battlefield Tour 'Totalize'
WO171 (War Diaries)
/640, 33rd Armoured Brigade
/680, 154th Infantry Brigade
/859, 1st Northants Yeomanry
/878, 144th RAC
/1265, 1st Black Watch
WO179/3010, War Diary, Sherbrooke Fusiliers

The Tank Museum, Bovington
RH 88, War Diary and Associated Notes, 144th RAC
Taped interview with Trooper Ekins

PRIMARY SOURCES (PUBLISHED)

Meyer, Kurt, *Grenadiers* (Winnipeg: J.J. Fedorowicz, 1994)

SECONDARY SOURCES (BOOKS)

Agte, Patrick, *Michael Wittmann and the Tiger Commanders of the Leibstandarte*, (Winnipeg, Ma.: J.J. Fedorowicz, 1996)

Chamberlain, Peter and Chris Ellis, *PzKpfW VI Tiger and Tiger I* (Profile AFV Series No. 48) (Windsor: Profile, 1972)

Fletcher, David, *Tiger! The Tiger Tank: A British View* (London: HMSO, 1986)

Ford, Roger, *Tiger Panzer* (Erlangen: Karl Müller Verlag, 1998)

Fortin, Ludovic, *British Tanks in Normandy* (Caen: Histoire & Collections, 2005)

Gander, Terry J., *Tanks in Detail: Medium Tank M4 (76mm and 105mm) Sherman and Firefly* (Hersham, Ian Allen, 2003)

Hart, Stephen A., 'Teenaged Nazi Warriors: The Fanaticism of the 12th SS Panzer Division *Hitlerjugend* in Normandy', in M. Hughes and G. Johnson (eds.), *Fanaticism and Modern Conflict* (London: Frank Cass, 2005)

Jentz, Thomas, L., *Germany's Tiger Tanks – Tigers I and II: Combat Tactics* (Atglen, PA: Schiffer, 1997)

Jentz, Thomas, L., Doyle, Hilary and Sarson, Peter, *Tiger I Heavy Tank 1942–45* (Oxford: Osprey Publishing, 1993)

Hayward, Mark, *Sherman Firefly* (Tiptree: Barbarossa Books, 2001)

Lupfer, Craig W.H., *Blood and Honor: The History of the 12th SS Panzer Division 'Hitler Youth', 1943–45* (San Jose, CA.: R. James Bender, 1987)

Meyer, Hubert, *Kriegsgeschichte der 12SS-Panzerdivision 'Hitlerjugend'* (Osnabrück: Munin verlag, 1982); in translation as *History of the 12-SS Panzer Division 'Hitlerjugend'* (Winnipeg: J.J. Fedorowicz, 1994)

Neville, R.F., *The 1st and 2nd Northants Yeomanry 1939–46* (Brunswick: Joh. Heinr. Meyer, 1946)

Reid, Brian A., *No Holding Back: Operation 'Totalize', Normandy, August 1944* (Toronto: Robin Brass, 2005)

Schneider, Wolfgang, *Panzertaktik: German Small-Unit Armor Tactics* (Winnipeg: J.J. Fedorowicz, 2000)

Spielberger, Walter J., *Tiger and King Tiger Tanks* (Sparkford: Haynes, 1991)

SECONDARY SOURCES (ARTICLES)

Abbott, John 'Bud', '1st Northamptonshire Yeomanry, St. Aignan', *Military Illustrated*, No. 69 (February 1994), pp 12–18

Niemis, Renato, 'Death of Wittmann', *Military Illustrated*, No. 132 (May 1999), pp 14–19

Taylor, Les, 'Michael Wittmann's Last Battle', *After the Battle*, No. 48 (1985), pp 46–53

INDEX